Direct Funding from a Southern Perspective

INTRAC NGO Management and Policy Series

1. *Institutional Development and NGOs in Africa: Policy Perspectives for European Development Agencies* Alan Fowler with Piers Campbell and Brian Pratt

2. *Governance, Democracy and Conditionality: What Role for NGOs?* Edited by Andrew Clayton

3. *Measuring the Process: Guidelines for Evaluating Social Development* David Marsden, Peter Oakley and Brian Pratt

4. *Strengthening the Capacity of NGOs: Cases of Small Enterprise Development Agencies in Africa* Caroline Sahley

5. *NGOs, Civil Society and the State: Building Democracy in Transitional Countries* Edited by Andrew Clayton

6. *Outcomes and Impact: Evaluating Change in Social Development* Peter Oakley, Brian Pratt and Andrew Clayton

7. *Demystifying Organisation Development: Practical Capacity-Building Experiences of African NGOs* Rick James

8. *Direct Funding from a Southern Perspective: Strengthening Civil Society?*

Direct Funding from a Southern Perspective:

Strengthening Civil Society?

INTRAC NGO Management and Policy Series No. 8

An INTRAC Publication

INTRAC:

The International Non-governmental Organisation Training and Research Centre

A Summary Description

INTRAC was set up in 1991 to provide specially designed management, training and research services for NGOs involved in relief and development in the South and dedicated to improving organisational effectiveness and programme performance of Northern NGOs and Southern partners where appropriate. Our goal is to serve NGOs in (i) the exploration of the management, policy and human resource issues affecting their own organisational development, and (ii) the evolution of more effective programmes of institutional development and cooperation.

INTRAC offers the complementary services of:
Training;
Consultancy; and
Research

First published in 1998 in the UK by
INTRAC
PO Box 563
Oxford
OX2 6RZ
United Kingdom

Tel: +44 (0)1865 201851
Fax: +44 (0)1865 201852
e-mail: intrac@gn.apc.org

ISBN 1-897748-26-4

Designed and produced by
Davies Burman Associates
Tel: 01865 343131

Printed in Great Britain by
Antony Rowe Ltd., Chippenham, Wiltshire

Contents

Acronyms

ADAB	Association of Development Agencies in Bangladesh
ADB	Asian Development Bank
AMREF	African Medical and Research Foundation
ASA ·	Association for Social Advancement (Bangladesh)
AKRSP	Aga Khan Rural Support Programme
BELA	Bangladesh Environmental Lawyers Association
BNP	Bangladesh National Party
BRAC	Bangladesh Rural Assistance Committee
CADEC	Catholic Development Commission (Zimbabwe)
CARE	Co-operation for Assistance and Relief Everywhere
CBO	community-based organisation
CCK	Christian Council of Kenya (later re-named NCCK)
CGAP	Consultative Group to Assist the Poorest (Bangladesh)
CIDA	Canadian International Development Agency
CIDRA	Coordindora Interinstitucinal para a Desarrollo Rural de Ayacucho (Peru)
CIS	Commonwealth of Independent States
CLARION	Centre for Law and Research International (Kenya)
COTU	Central Organisation of Trade Unions (Kenya)
CPK	Church of the Province of Kenya
CRS	Catholic Relief Services
CUSO	Canadian University Service Overseas
DAC	Development Assistance Committee
DANIDA	Danish International Development Agency
DDC	District Development Committees (Kenya)
DFID	Department for International Development (UK)
EC	European Community
EU	European Union
FONCODES	Fondo Nacional de Compensacion y Desarrollo Social (Peru)
FPAK	Family Planning Association Kenya
GDP	gross domestic product
GK	Gonoshystha Kendra (Bangladesh)
GSS	Gono Shahajjo Sangstha (Bangladesh)

IDPAA	Institute for Development Policy, Analysis and Advocacy (Bangladesh)
IDB	Inter-American Development Bank
IFI	International financial institution
IMF	International Monetary Fund
INFEP	Integrated Non-Formal Education Project
ITDG	Intermediate Technology Development Group
KANU	Kenya Africa National Union
KENGO	Kenya Energy and Environmental Organisation
KPU	Kenya People's Union
K-REP	Kenya Rural Enterprise Programme
NAB	NGO National Affairs Bureau (Bangladesh)
NCCK	see CCK
NGO	non-governmental organisation
NGOSC	Non-Governmental Organisation Standing Committee (Kenya)
NORAD	Norwegian Development Agency
NOVIB	Nederlandse Organisatie voor Internationale Ontwikkelilgssamenwerking (Netherlands Organisation for International Development Co-operation)
NCPD	National Council for Population Development (Kenya)
ODA	Overseas Development Administration (UK, now DFID)
ODA	Official Development Assistance
ODI	Overseas Development Institute
OECD	Organization for Economic Co-operation and Development
PAC	Partnership Africa Canada
PCGCF	Peru and Canada General Counterpart Fund
PKSF	Palli Karma Shahayak Foundaition (Bangladesh)
PVO	Private Voluntary Organisation
RCP	Rural Credit Programme (Bangladesh)
RDP	Rural Development Programme (Bangladesh)
RDRS	Rangpur-Dinajpur Rural Development Service (Bangladesh)
SDD	Social Dimension of Development (Kenya)
SECTI	Secretariat for International Technical Co-operation (Peru)
SIDA	Swedish International Development Agency
UN	United Nations
UNDP	United Nations Development Programme
UNICEF	United Nations Children's Fund
USAID	US Agency for International Development
WID	Women in Development
WUSC	World University Service of Canada

Preface

A common limitation of many studies of the aid system is that they are focused on the past and frequently on those elements which have not worked. Findings and recommendations are often dated by the time they are published and the debate has been overtaken by events. The present study has tried over almost two years to track an accelerating trend towards a shift in official funding from northern to southern NGOs. We sought to take a southern perspective of this trend and to complement previous work which has more clearly come with a northern parentage. During the study we have tried to test our ideas as they developed through workshops in some of the case study countries and through a consultation in Denmark as well as other seminars and discussions in several countries.

The study has encompassed a large number of people at different points. It was initiated by Brian Pratt and Alan Fowler, who then continued to be involved in its realisation, and early investigation was assisted by Sara Gibbs. Later Raj Patel and Lars Jorgensen worked together on setting up the case studies and refining the research questions. In-country research and the case study writing was carried out by Patrick Osodo (Kenya), Teobaldo Pinzas (Peru) and Babar Sobhan (Bangladesh). Supplementary material was supplied by Simon Matsvai (Zimbabwe). Throughout the process Ian Smillie provided advice. Further writing and editing was provided by Janet Danziger (Peru) and Simon Heap (Kenya), and the text was finalised by Firoze Manji, Brian Pratt and Jillian Popkins. Many other people assisted in the case study research, some of whom are listed in the full case studies, and we owe them all a special thanks for their time and ideas.

The methodology we used is described in the Appendices. Further details of the case studies are available in four Occasional Papers already published by INTRAC: *Partners or Contractors? Official Donor Agencies and Direct Funding Mechanisms: Three Northern Case Studies – CIDA, EU and USAID* by Ian Smillie, Francis Douxchamps and Rebecca Sholes/Jane Covey, OPS 11 (1996); *Partners or Contractors? The Relationship between Official Agencies and NGOs – Bangladesh* by Babar Sobhan, OPS 14 (1997); *Partners or Contractors? The Relationship between Official Agencies and NGOs – Peru* by Teobaldo Pinzas, OPS 15 (1997); *Partners or Contractors? The Relationship between Official Agencies and NGOs – Kenya and Zimbabwe* by Patrick Osodo and Simon Matsvai OPS 16 (1998). A limited distribution report was written on the consultative meeting with northern official agencies and NGOs 'Changing Relations between Donors and Southern NGOs', October 1996.

Thanks are due to those willing to support a study into what has been regarded as a controversial area, primarily the Ford Foundation and Danchurchaid, with support for the consultative meeting from DANIDA.

We feel that the present overview has captured the essence of the many points made to us in the case study countries as well as in our interviews with donors in several European and North America countries.

Brian Pratt
Oxford June 1998

Introduction

This book presents evidence that the use of direct funding as an instrument for aid has transformed relationships between key players in the development world. Direct funding is a practice in which an official donor provides financial assistance to a non-governmental organisation (NGO) without the involvement of an intermediary such as another NGO or a local government agency. Since the late 1980s an increase in both the volume and incidence of direct funding has changed the international funding environment, bringing qualitative changes to relations between the people, organisations and institutions involved with the international development system. This book raises questions regarding what changes in funding patterns and the advent of direct funding in particular mean for:

- the relationship between northern and southern NGOs;
- the relationships between official donors and southern NGOs;
- the respective stakeholders of the changes in funding patterns.

Recent changes in funding patterns reflect shifts in the dominant model of development assistance. In the post-colonial era, it was assumed that southern governments would play a central role in both the management of the economy and the provision of social services. By the 1980s, this optimism had given way to frustration as, in the wake of the debt crisis, country after country experienced economic stagnation and a decline in the quality and availability of social services, especially to the poor. The 1980s was a period which saw growing disenchantment with the state as the vehicle of development. This disenchantment was the political interface to the ideology that free trade, free enterprise and the growth of the private sector were necessary preconditions for successful development. However, under structural adjustment neither the fledgeling private sector nor the discredited state could be depended upon to deliver services to the poor. The search for alternative mechanisms led to the NGO sector.

The practice of providing significant amounts of aid funding through the NGO sector in the South was neither a sudden nor a conscious choice. It emerged out of diverse empirical experience in the delivery of aid funding across different countries. There was no theoretical treatise established a priori to justify the shift in praxis: the rationale for engaging in direct funding was developed after the fact. Despite their disillusionment with the state, northern official agencies were eager to continue to support development efforts in the South. Bilateral agencies such as Swedish International Development Agency (SIDA) and Canadian International Development Agency (CIDA) began to explore the possibility of identifying new and more effective vehicles for their development assistance; the most obvious candidates were the growing number of local NGOs and community-based organisations (CBOs) which were perceived to constitute civil society in the South.

The first chapter outlines recent trends in funding to the NGO sector. It summarises the rationale behind direct funding from the perspective of the donor agencies and illustrates associated funding practices. The three case studies which follow detail southern perspectives on experience of direct funding.[1] In the subsequent chapter there is an analysis of the impact of direct funding on relationships within the NGO sector and between it and official agencies. This analysis generates certain management implications for each of the three groups (southern NGOs, northern NGOs and donor agencies) which are explored in the final chapter.

Despite the different histories described in the case studies, there are striking similarities in the effect that direct funding in the 1990s has had on the non-governmental sector. The main findings of this study demonstrate that:

- funding patterns have strongly influenced, if not distorted, the shape and form of civil society;
- the advent of direct funding has placed pressure on NGOs to act as subcontractors, performing the delivery of specific services defined by donors; and
- northern NGOs have come under pressure to reinvent themselves as intermediaries in the subcontracting chain, rather than working as agents of change in solidarity with their southern partners.

This research initiative complements existing work on the effects of NGO–donor relations in two important ways. First, by concentrating on the experience and perspectives of NGOs in the South, it redresses the bias towards northern perspectives displayed by most existing studies.[2] Secondly, it includes the civic as well as the operational dimensions of NGOs, recognising that supporting the NGO contribution to civil society is an explicit objective of direct funding.

---

[1] See Appendix 1 for an outline of research methodology.
[2] i.e. OECD 1996a; Randel and German 1996, 1997; ODI 1995.

The research process itself, which involved a study of at least thirty-five NGOs in each case study country and a comprehensive review of donor activities, has generated considerable interest. Most NGOs have been very willing to talk about changes in funding. The majority of official agencies sought to provide information and to enter the debate, regarding participation in the research as means of improving their funding practices. Many of those who were interviewed, or attended workshops, were remarkably candid about changes in their own institutions and how funding patterns and policies are affecting the way they work. In particular, there was evidence that NGOs put considerable thought into the implications of global funding trends for their organisations.

It is the purpose of this book to offer food for thought and to invite donors, whether NGOs or official agencies, to take a critical look at their use of direct funding. In transforming the relationships of key players, direct funding has also contributed to a shift in the development environment. The use and management of direct funding and the nature of the relations which this engenders locates donors on a spectrum of development activity. At one end of this spectrum is service delivery, which tends to emphasise the efficient administration of aid. At the other is a community development approach, which is characterised by strong ties with local groups. If the increased incidence of direct funding exerts a pull towards one then the shape of the sector is changed. This has implications for both the capacity and the legitimacy of the sector as a whole to perform a wide range of diverse activities.

In the final analysis the case studies illustrate that change cannot be entirely attributed to the use of a specific funding mechanism (i.e. direct funding). This study locates the role direct funding has played in the context of changes in the political economy of development and in development policies pursued by northern governments and multilateral agencies in the 1980s and 1990s. Direct funding is an established feature of the aid landscape which has yet to be fully consolidated and understood. This study should therefore be considered as an opportunity to pause for reflection. The practical implications of direct funding are still emerging and many of the best practices identified through this exercise remain isolated incidences.

Chapter 1

Direct Funding

FUNDING TRENDS: FACTS AND FIGURES

Since the 1980s, an increasing proportion of official development assistance has been channelled to the NGO sector (OECD 1993; ODI 1995). By the mid-1990s, northern governments' annual contributions to NGOs had reached approximately US$1 billion. The proportion of aid funds directed by the Organization for Economic Co-operation and Development (OECD) countries to NGOs has varied, with Japan providing only 1%, and Sweden 30% in the mid-1990s. The degree of dependency of northern NGOs on funds from official donor sources has also varied: for example, in the mid-1990s Swedish NGOs, obtained 85% of their total income from official aid sources, whereas UK NGOs obtained only about 10% (ODI 1995).

This growth in funding to the NGO sector has occurred during a period in which there has been an overall reduction of total aid contributions from OECD countries from US$59,610 million in 1992 to US$55,114 million in 1996 (Randel and German 1997). In total some US$6 billion a year has been disbursed through NGOs since 1992. An increasing proportion of this is earmarked for emergency relief and assistance (OECD 1996).

Research indicated that although almost all of the official agencies reviewed are increasing their funding of NGOs, in most other areas declining levels of financial assistance account for an overall fall in levels of aid. Danish International Development Agency (DANIDA) and the European Union (EU) are the only exceptions, with increases in the levels of their aid commitments. The country studies for this research show that significant funds are now available out of decentralised bilateral programmes which are not measurable at headquarters. This represents one of several different mechanisms which are collectively defined as direct funding. Some examples are given in Box 1.1.

To fully understand the volume and incidence of direct funding of southern organisations it is necessary to disaggregate information with greater clarity and consistency than is common across bilateral and multilateral donor agencies. It is difficult to isolate the volume of funding channelled through each mechanism from funding statistics expressed in the aggregate. For example, making accurate assessments of the amounts disbursed through NGOs for a specific theme, such as non-emergency related development work, is difficult. Each country has different ways of reporting allocations and applies different criteria for categorising specific aid budget lines.[1] Several methodological limitations relating to statistical information emerged during the research process:

- many donors only record funds allocated to NGO Co-Financing Programmes[2] and therefore a significant proportion of bilateral official development assistance (ODA), channelled through NGOs, is not reported in Development Assistance Committee (DAC) statistics;

- aid statistics may not isolate amounts channelled *through* NGOs (as part of subcontracting the official aid programme) from money donated *to* NGOs (as co-financing, for example);

- in their data handling systems, official agencies tend not to distinguish between funding to northern and southern NGOs;

- funds allocated for Food Aid or Emergency Aid (which are increasingly being channelled through NGOs) may not be recorded separately from funds for development;

- there is untimely reporting of figures by some donors resulting in their omission from the statistics for a number of years. For example, the 1995 figures of total ODA channelled through NGOs by member countries of DAC does not include contributions to NGOs by the USA (which appear as nil or negligible on their statistical tables);

- systems for co-ordination and information exchange between ministries/head offices and embassies/field offices or between various field offices are often weak, leading to missing data on disbursements.

---

[1] Because of these limitations, in particular the untimely reporting of figures and the difficulty of knowing how each agency's figures are calculated, figures in this text have remained in the currency in which they were reported. It was felt that to convert the figures would encourage comparison on a false basis. The issue of the difficulty of making accurate comparisons is an important one in its own right.

[2] Under co-financing funding regimes, NGOs receive a proportion of funding from an official agency and are required to 'match' that with their own fund-raising to meet the budget.

Box 1.1: Mechanisms of Direct Funding

Type of funding	Aim of funding	Funding mechanism
Ambassador Fund	To build good relations with local communities by providing limited occasional support to small civic organisations and NGOs.	Amounts are generally small (a few thousand US dollars), given to buy small items of equipment or to support discrete events. Process is straightforward, with few, if any, conditions. Discretionary fund, administered in-country by ambassador. E.g. a new cooker for the local orphanage.
Thematic Funds	To promote specific official agency priorities, for example gender equality, human rights or small enterprise development.	Budget with an upper limit allocated over a period of time. Funds project costs. Decisions on the way they are administered are taken in-country by representatives of the official agency. E.g. CIDA has a fund entitled 'equity agenda' for promotion of gender awareness.
Bilateral Official Development Co-operation	To fulfil the aims of a country framework agreement made between governments.	Large amounts of money involved spread over several years, for example DFID's donation of US$ 12 million to BRAC 1991–3. Funds most often allocated to projects within larger programmes with a focus on cost-effective delivery (some consideration may be given to NGO's capacity-building needs). Funding decisions made jointly by local offices and relevant ministries in the North. An increasing number of agencies are offering a mixed range of funds to governments, private sector and NGOs as a way of achieving a single goal.

Box 1.1 (continued)

Type of funding	Aim of funding	Funding mechanism
Multilateral Official Development Co-operation	To fulfil the aims of country framework agreements made with multilateral organisations. These are: 1. United Nations (UN) system, e.g. UNDP; 2. International financial institutions (IFI), e.g. the World Bank.	1. Co-implement aid projects using their own finance and expertise. Government approval is usually required for UN–NGO agreements and may involve ministry infrastructure such as primary health care clinics. 2. Governments must be the legal recipient and guarantor of repayment of funds from IFIs. NGOs can be the designated recipients of IFI loans via the government. This is particularly the case with world development funds. The World Bank now publishes a guide for NGOs wishing to participate in World Bank funded programmes, although these are tied to actual or potential loans.
Counterpart Funds	To supply a country with funding through monetisation of food aid, proceeds from sale of machinery or other goods provided by official agencies.	Funds distributed by various means with official agency maintaining significant decision-making powers.
Delegated Funds	To support NGO sector.	Funds established by NGO divisions for allocation within specific NGO networks. Funding from NNGOs is redistributed to SNGOs.

9

The need for DAC to standardise definitions and methods when collating statistics from member countries was noted in a joint meeting between OECD member country bilateral agencies and the northern NGO sector in 1993 (Smillie and Helmich 1993).

TRENDS IN OFFICIAL AID TO THE NGO SECTOR IN THE 1990s[3]

As has been noted, official aid has declined for most agencies, the exceptions being Denmark (whose contribution has risen from US$1.3 billion in 1993 to US$ 1.8 billion in 1996) and the European Commission (whose budget has grown rapidly from US$1,244 million in 1980–1 to US$7,100 million in 1995). For example, SIDA's official aid contributions have declined from US$2,460 million in 1992 to US$1,968 million in 1996, representing 0.82% of GNP, near-ly its lowest level for 20 years (OECD 1996; Randel and German 1997). British aid contributions declined from 0.31% of GNP in 1994 to 0.27% in 1996, and US Agency for International Development (USAID) disbursements have declined during the 1990s, from US$11,709 million (or 0.18% of GNP) to US$9,058 million (or 0.12% of GNP) in 1996 (OECD 1996; Randel and German, 1997).

At the same time the proportion of funds available to NGOs has increased. The proportion of funds provided to the NGO sector (Private Voluntary Organisations and southern NGOs) by USAID, for example, increased from US$496 million in 1991 to US$675.5 million in 1995. Commitment to funding NGOs was articulated in US Vice-President Al Gore's pledge at the 1995 Social Summit, that the US government 'would seek to channel up to 40% of its assis-tance to poor countries through private aid and charity groups that have demon-strated greater efficiency than many international organizations including the United Nations' (*Washington Post*, 13 March 1995).

The proportion of funding to the NGO sector in the North has grown. For example, resources to NGOs provided by DFID through the Joint Funding Scheme have increased from US$ 44.8 million in 1992–3 to US$57.6 million in 1995–6 (DFID 1997) and in 1995 funds provided to Danish NGOs by DANIDA amounted to 16.5% of the bilateral budget. The European Commission began funding European development NGOs in 1976 with an allocation of US$2.66 million, and the programme has grown substantially since, reaching US$856 million in 1994 (Cox and Koning 1997).

The picture for direct funding has also been one of a growing share of the

---

[3] See Appendix 2 for more detailed information.

declining total. Between 1981 and 1994 the Norwegian Development Agency (NORAD) disbursement through direct funding rose from US$250, 000 in 1981 to US$14.5 million in 1993. Direct funding was introduced by DANIDA in 1988 and in general has been set at 10% of total aid financing for any individual country. The volume of USAID direct funding has grown from US$184 million in 1991 to US$307.8 million in 1995. Even the World Bank, which provides the vast majority of its development assistance to governments in the form of loans, has funded NGOs directly through its Emergency Social Funds. There are also small grants made to support activities designed to promote dialogue. In 1995 the World Bank made awards totalling US$500,000 to 40 organisations world-wide. In the same year, southern NGOs received 80% of the total.[4]

In general it is the larger NGOs in the South that have benefited from direct funding. Several bilateral programmes made substantial grants to a small number of large southern NGOs. For example, Bangladesh Rural Advancement Committee (BRAC, in Bangladesh) received US$12 million between 1991 and 1993, Aga Khan Rural Support Programme (AKRSP, in Pakistan) received US$5.7 million between 1987 and 1991 from DFID. CIDA has in the past provided substantial grants to support certain larger NGOs in the south directly, from its bilateral programme, one of the first being Proshika in Bangladesh. In principle, southern NGOs have access to funds under certain line items of the EC budget, but with a small number of exceptions, few southern NGOs have been able to obtain funds, partly as a consequence of the cumbersome procedures involved. Consequently the EC has shared the tendency to fund only large NGOs which are already strong. Small amounts of funds are disbursed to NGOs through embassies: such as the British embassies in South Asia, Kenya and South Africa, or Canadian embassies which administer small grants for southern NGOs.

OFFICIAL AID AGENCY RATIONALE FOR DIRECT FUNDING

The predominant view amongst official aid agencies has been that building democracy and pluralism requires a robust civil society, and the provision of funds to NGOs represents additional resources for strengthening civil society. In many countries, it is believed, lack of political freedom, absence of parliamentary democracy and violation of human rights constitute real obstacles to development. Freedom of the individual as well as free enterprise are viewed as

---

[4] These statistics give no indication of the *degree* of NGO involvement with social funds, which can vary greatly. Malena (1997) estimates that approximately '15% of total social fund disbursements are channelled through NGOs'.

the corner-stones of development. From the point of view of official aid agencies, direct funding enables local organisations to influence the state and create a much needed dialogue. They have sought therefore to focus attention on supporting initiatives related to governance, human rights and democracy, as well as stimulating the growth of the private sector. In this respect, reducing the volume of funding to government and increasing support to the NGO sector was perceived as a means of consolidating the influence of northern governments through their respective aid agencies. It was accepted by most agencies that involvement in and support for civil society includes some degree of political influence, although this is frequently expressed as promotion of good governance or the need to find ways to counterbalance the inefficiencies of the state.

Most official aid agencies believed that NGOs had a better track record than the state when it came to poverty-based development work and felt, therefore, that reaching the poor would be more effectively achieved by directing aid towards the NGO sector. Much of the attention of donor agencies had been directed towards supporting economic structural adjustment programmes. But at the same time, in an attempt to mitigate the impact of such programmes on the poor, they believed that certain basic services to the most vulnerable sections of society needed to be provided. NGOs provided an important mechanism for ensuring that basic services reached the most vulnerable sectors in society in a way that was more effective and considerably cheaper than funding development initiatives through the public sector. NGOs were perceived, therefore, as being able to deliver value for money. There was also a belief that the NGO sector was creative and innovative, and that links with the community made NGOs more accountable to target groups than the public sector. Furthermore, support to the southern NGO sector put official agencies, they believed, in a position to learn more about local conditions and to gain important insights about ways of improving the quality of aid.

It was this mixture of pragmatism and ideology which rationalised the adoption of the NGO sector by donor agencies as an alternative partner to the state. NGOs appeared to be more effective and efficient than states (government) which were commonly condemned as bureaucratised labyrinthine structures, often unresponsive, corrupt, inefficient and unreliable. The high failure rate of government projects supported this image. For the same reasons, many official aid agencies believed that the state's involvement in the economy needed to be reduced, and the role of the private sector ought to be encouraged as the motor of development. Support for the NGO sector was viewed very much as part of a dual strategy of reducing the ubiquity of the state in economic matters and encouraging the private sector. Support to NGOs as well as the state was designed to send a strong message not only to the government, but also to the southern NGO sector and its constituencies, to counter the negative way in which the North has been regarded in the past.

In addition, some donor agencies believed that northern NGOs added a superfluous management layer, accruing costs in the implementation of projects which could be avoided through direct funding. There were doubts raised by some about the value added by northern NGOs. Frequently, they felt, northern NGOs were engaged in advocacy and campaigning in a way that detracted from their usefulness in the implementation of projects which were of interest or concern to the official agency. Aid agencies were, nevertheless, sensitive to their own voting public, and while there may be perceived advantages to providing funding directly to poverty related projects, they were also aware that northern NGOs did not always welcome the fact that their roles as intermediaries were being reduced.

Donor country opinion strongly affected the extent to which the official agencies promoted direct funding. NORAD, for example, has faced considerable pressure at home to withdraw from direct funding of southern NGOs. A review of Norway's development policies concluded: 'NORAD should consider gradually terminating its support for local NGOs, because of foreign policy considerations and problems related to power structures, sustainability and organisational cultures ... If the aim is to use the local organisations for specific political purposes, which is an idea that goes against Norwegian traditional relationships with these countries, then this should be the task of the Foreign Ministry rather than NORAD' (Tvedt 1995).

In a comparable report the British Overseas Development Administration (ODA, now Department for International Development) expressed a different attitude towards political life in the South. 'ODA should broaden the objectives it has for interacting with southern NGOs well beyond those of enhancing the efficiency and effectiveness of the British aid programme. Thus, where country-specific circumstances deem it appropriate, interaction should strive, additionally, to strengthen civil society [in order to] promote sustainable economic and social development and good government' (Riddell and Bebbington 1995). The Norwegian report questions whether it is appropriate for an aid agency to interfere in politics but in the British report, the good government agenda justifies intervention. However, both reports agree that there is a stark link between directly funding civil society organisations and promoting a political programme.

CIVIL SOCIETY, NGOS AND DIRECT FUNDING

In the rhetoric of the good governance agenda, civil society is loosely defined as a collection of diverse organisational forms that exist outside of the state and the market. Some are politically active and in dialogue with, or in opposition to, the state. Others aim at supplying segments of society with social services not provided by the state, while others again are recreational or meeting places for people with similar interests. The growth in direct funding sought to feed resources into this strata of society. By so doing it was assumed to be enhancing individual freedoms and facilitating the establishment of pluralist democracy: factors perceived to be the key to the growth of the private sector and free enterprise.

Foreign donors have in general underestimated the complexity of civil society in individual countries and failed to recognise that many of the functions of civil society are already being fulfilled, or have the potential to be fulfilled, by existing structures or systems. They have been unable or unwilling to look beyond Western liberal notions of civil society and have directed funding at the new NGOs, overlooking other types of organisation (including local government). For example, in Vietnam NGOs are a relatively new type of organisation, which have been strongly supported by external donors. Consequently, poorly developed links with local communities put legitimacy into question and some NGOs are seen by Vietnamese people as profit-making or foreign organisations (Harper 1996).

Some official agencies recognise that development NGOs are not the only actors within civil society. For example, USAID explicitly includes a wide range of organisations within civil society such as professional associations, community organisations and labour unions. However, none of the official donors seems to have a clear policy on which organisations within civil society they support. An evaluation of NORAD's support for NGOs concludes that funding decisions are made largely on an *ad hoc* basis (Tvedt 1995). This conclusion seems to be widely applicable to other official agencies. Furthermore, the requirement that recipient organisations fulfil certain formal legal and financial criteria tends to favour support for development NGOs at the expense of other civil society organisations. Many of the latter may not meet these formal organisational conditions yet they may play an equally valid role in local civil society.

The potential for direct funding to serve as a means of strengthening civil society also depends on an understanding of the relationship between it and the state. Many commentators have argued that civil society needs a strong state, both at a central and local level, in order to flourish, and vice versa. Tordoff (1994) writes, 'If democracy is to become a reality ... it is necessary to breathe life into the formal institutions which have been created and to strengthen civil society.' In other words, civil society and the state need not necessarily be in competition for a limited amount of power in a zero-sum game, but rather that they can both be mutually reinforcing. In its earliest form (i.e. in Bangladesh) little or no consideration was given to the likely effect that direct funding would have on relations between the government and NGOs. Most donors at the time tended to view the two relationships as discreet interactions with no, or very little, overlap. Funding for NGOs remained relatively healthy in the context of declining volumes of aid, resulting in the perception that more funds for NGOs meant fewer funds for government.

For southern governments the new relationship between official agencies and NGOs has posed a range of challenges and opportunities. In a study of NGO–state relations in three African countries, Bratton (1989) notes the inherent tensions between a government's need for order and control and an NGO's desire for organisational autonomy. He argued that a government's relationship with domestic NGOs is defined more by concerns of national sovereignty and regime stability, and less by economic and social considerations. Hence, where the regime fears for its own legitimacy, the likelihood of it being amenable to the work of NGOs is severely reduced.

It is in the context of the political economy of aid that the growth in funds channelled directly to southern NGOs has had an immediate and obvious impact. With the growth of direct funding NGOs began to encroach on the role of governments as the principal partners of official agencies, and enjoyed a degree of confidence and influence that had been unimaginable a few years previously. At the same time, government ministries were being heavily criticised as overly bureaucratic and out of touch with the needs of the poor. Direct funding enabled some southern NGOs to increase the scale of their activities significantly, while apparently demonstrating that this could be achieved at lower cost than that of the public sector and without any apparent decline in the quality of the services provided. In these respects it appeared that direct funding was a highly successful innovation in development practice. The infusion of official funds had a dramatic impact on the work of southern NGOs. From having led a hand-to-mouth existence, they suddenly found themselves with the resources to purchase the latest technology and equipment, to attract quality staff with higher salaries and to invest in physical infrastructure. In Bangladesh, Sobhan (1990) has described how an entire class has emerged whose ability to reproduce itself is entirely dependent on its capacity to control the use and distribution of foreign aid.

The rhetoric of good governance and its representation of civil society has failed to understand the diverse forms civil society can take in particular contexts, to distinguish between different organisations and the contribution they make to civil society and to understand the complex relationship between state and civil society. What the three case studies that follow show is that these are all areas on which the operationalisation of direct funding has had a profound impact. By examining what happened in a particular country from the perspective of each we can see how direct funding has exerted pressure on the nature and shape of civil society.

Chapter 2

Bangladesh: Partners or Contractors

NGOS IN BANGLADESH

NGO involvement in Bangladesh dates back to the 1970 cyclone that devastated the coastal areas of the country and the War of Independence in 1971. Northern NGOs, such as OXFAM and Co-operation for Assistance and Relief Everywhere (CARE), undertook extensive relief work in partnership with a few local organisations as Bangladesh attempted to reconstruct its shattered economy, following a conflict that destroyed virtually all the country's infrastructure as well as causing massive social upheavals. As it became clear that Bangladesh's problems ran deeper than simple relief, organisations such as BRAC began to re-orient their work towards more long-term development focus.

In doing so, many NGOs were strongly influenced by the work of the Comilla Rural Development Project, a government project targeted at farmer co-operatives, aimed at spreading the use of green revolution technology during the 1960s. NGOs quickly came to the realisation, however, that such community development projects were helping the relatively well-off farmers in rural Bangladesh, often to the detriment of the landless poor whose labour power was being replaced by mechanised forms of farming. This realisation, coupled with the growing influence of Paulo Freire's book, *The Pedagogy of the Oppressed* (1970), motivated a shift away from the extension model of development. NGOs began to analyse poverty not simply in terms of a lack of resources, but also in terms of a lack of access to power at the grass-roots level. Many NGOs consequently adopted an empowerment model of development, with emphasis on social mobilisation and conscientisation through education and training.

By the 1980s, these same NGOs were finding it increasingly difficult to sustain projects due to a lack of sufficient mass support. This was caused in part by the fact that their beneficiaries continued to be economically marginalised. Many of the larger NGOs began to explore the use of credit and income-generation projects combined with the provision of basic health and educational services in what has come to be known as the integrated rural development model. This was seen as a necessary step on the path to empowerment. This is not to suggest that there was wholesale rejection of the philosophy of social mobilisation, but rather to indicate a shift in perspective that was, in large part, based on pragmatism and the NGO sectorís assessment of its own comparative advantage *vis-à-vis* the state. The experiment with grass-roots mobilisation was not a failure: NGOs learned valuable lessons about reaching and working with the very poor. Using limited resources, local NGOs demonstrated that alternatives did exist to the seemingly ineffective state bureaucracies.

The emergence of an indigenous development actor outside the state sector took place at a time when donors were becoming increasingly frustrated with government performance in the delivery of basic services to the poor. Faced with the option of ending development assistance or finding an alternative, some donors began to work directly with NGOs in the early 1980s. This trend increased in the subsequent decade. Resources available to the NGOs grew from approximately 6% of total foreign aid disbursement in 1988–9 to an average of 17% by 1995. The number of NGO projects increased tenfold over the same period. By the mid-1990s there were few areas of the country that did not have some sort of local NGO presence. The ubiquity and success of local NGOs so penetrated the consciousness of the country that it became increasingly common for other civil society actors to recast themselves as NGOs.

By 1997, there were approximately 16,000 societies and organisations registered under the Societies Act. This number included a wide variety of groups ranging from the smallest civic organisations to international NGOs. Of these, about 756 were registered with the NGO National Affairs Bureau (NAB) and were thus eligible to receive foreign funding. Of that group, around thirty NGOs receive about 80% of all funds channelled through the sector, 60% of which went to the largest NGOs (ADAB/PACT). A similar pattern was also apparent with respect to the distribution of funds from direct funding channels.

The distribution of the NGOs in Bangladesh has been geographically uneven. Although NGOs were present in about 75% of all Thanas,[1] the vast majority of their activities have been concentrated in Dhaka Division, an area which accounts for 31% of the population.

NGOS AND THE STATE

Historically, NGOs in Bangladesh have seen themselves as politically neutral or in opposition to the government. They have frequently operated in a harsh polit-

---

[1] Administrative areas, below district level.

ical and economic climate. In the early period, and typical of NGOs elsewhere, they almost always evaluated their performance in comparison with that of the public (state) sector. NGOs were usually quick to belittle government projects as inefficient, inappropriate, bureaucratic, centralised and non-participatory, especially when it became clear that there was a receptive audience in a donor community that was becoming increasingly frustrated by the lack of success of many government projects. There has always been friction between NGOs and the state, even where NGOs have co-operated with them in implementing projects. In a study of government–NGO co-operation in income-generating projects, Sanyal observed that:

> not only did they differ in their assessment of whether these projects were worthwhile and replicable, they were also critical of each other's roles in design and implementation ... yet these institutions continue to work together ... in antagonistic co-operation (Sanyal 1991)

Government officials (both political and in the state bureaucracy) have always been somewhat ambivalent about NGOs. While most would concede that NGOs have contributed to alleviating rural hardship, there has also been a tendency to try and control or co-opt the NGO movement, lest it reflected too negatively on the performance of the state. The creation of the NAB in 1989 by the then President Ershad was widely perceived as an attempt to bring the sector firmly under control. NGOs who wished to receive foreign funding had to register with, and have their projects approved by, NAB. In spite of NGO suspicions, obtaining NAB clearance turned out to be a routine procedure. But unease has remained about NAB's power to withhold approval of projects arbitrarily.

In 1992, the government sought to curb the growth and influence of the sector with new legislation that attempted to draw a distinction between NGOs and other civil society organisations. This move was vigorously opposed by the NGO community, alarmed by what it perceived as an attempt to create artificial distinctions and possibly sow divisions in civil society. At the height of the dispute, the licence of the Association of Development Agencies in Bangladesh (ADAB), the co-ordinating body for NGOs in Bangladesh, was temporarily withdrawn and only reinstated after the intervention of several foreign embassies. The government also used the conflict to accuse NGOs of supporting extravagant lifestyles and misusing funds meant for the poor. In practice, the government has been able to exercise far less control, although attempts have been made to impose arbitrary requirements on NGO programmes.

19

DONOR AGENCY FUNDING TO THE NGO SECTOR

Internationally, the vast majority of southern NGOs have received the bulk of their funds through northern NGOs, despite the availability of direct funding instruments. A large proportion of such funds originate, however, from bilateral sources, with the northern NGOs acting as intermediaries. In Bangladesh, however, direct funding of NGOs has surpassed the traditional route in volume of funds, importance and influence. On the surface there appears to be no inherent contradiction between direct funding and the relationship between northern and Bangladeshi NGOs. The traditional intermediary role played by northern NGOs has, however, come under scrutiny. For some time the annual budgets of large Bangladeshi NGOs including BRAC, Proshika and Gono Shahajjo Sangstha (GSS) have been in excess of US$10 million each and growing, well beyond the scope of even the best-endowed northern NGO. In 1997 BRAC's budget was over US$50 million and Proshika's budget for the period 1994–6 was US$175 million.[2] Furthermore, as the NGO sector in Bangladesh has matured, it has become far less reliant on northern NGOs for technical or operational expertise.

There has been tension between donors and NGOs on the issue of providing core funding as opposed to project funding. NGOs have argued that core funding (untied funds, the use of which is left to the discretion of the NGO) is crucial because it enables them to respond flexibly to the needs of the poor. Core funding is seen as necessary if the NGO institutions themselves are to develop adequate capacity and become sustainable. But underlying this debate is the NGO concern about who determines the development agenda. Untied core funds are seen as a means by which NGOs can make their own decisions about priorities. Project funds are necessarily tied to an agreement with the donor that only certain specific activities will be carried out over a given time period, the activities and timing being heavily influenced by the donor. NGOs have, therefore, certain suspicions that this places them closer to being subcontractors than partners. In addition, there is strong criticism about project funding being heavily influenced by fads and fashions in the donors' own countries, reflecting preoccupations that may be important to the taxpayers at home, but neglect the needs and concerns of the poor in Bangladesh. Core funding is seen as a means to delegate control over decision-making to the NGOs, reflecting a degree of trust on the donor's side that enhances partnership.

Bilateral donors are frequently reluctant to provide core funding since they

---

[2] The breakdown of Proshika's budget for Phase V (1994–6) is: EU ($33m), Proshika ($31.6m), DFID ($19.6m), CIDA ($11.5m), NOVIB ($8.6m), Ford Foundation ($6.7m), SIDA ($4m) and EZE ($3.5m). The remaining $73.2m comes from loan recoveries.

are often under pressure to demonstrate that they retain control of development aid funds and that they are used for activities that their taxpayers consider important. Staff training and development, training managers, constructing training centres, and similar activities are seen as unfashionable. NGOs argue, however, that these activities are important for building organisations that are able to serve the poor with any competence. The trend away from core funding has also touched the relationship between northern and southern NGOs, especially as northern NGOs have to rely increasingly on public campaigns for their funds: they find it easier to raise funds for specific projects (that, for example, put a child in school) than for abstract concepts such as capacity-building.

The donor community operating in Bangladesh is not homogeneous in its perception of priorities, preference for particular funding mechanisms or in the way individual donors wish to relate to NGOs. Each bilateral donor operates within the context of its own agenda for national development in Bangladesh. Broadly speaking, the donor community in Bangladesh can be divided into three main groups. CIDA, SIDA, NORAD and DANIDA have the longest experience with direct funding. They often collaborate informally as part of the Like-Minded Group. This group has traditionally been considered to represent the most progressive donors, who were willing to provide direct funding at a time when most bilateral donors were primarily focused on supporting government projects. The second group includes DFID and the EU, both of whom have more recently begun to channel funds through local NGOs, and are amongst the better endowed and increasingly influential members of the donor community. Amongst the multilateral donors the United Nations Development Programme (UNDP), the United Nations Children's Fund (UNICEF), and more recently the World Bank, have developed provisions for channelling funds to NGOs in Bangladesh.

There appears to be no set formula for explaining why different donors chose to venture down the path of direct funding. Some Bangladeshi NGOs had already begun the process of seeking substantial sources of funds as a means of expanding the scale of their activities, amounts that were probably beyond the capability of their northern partners to mobilise. Some degree of pragmatism and empiricism probably determined how each behaved. In the case of Sweden, Denmark and Norway, the move towards direct funding was probably prompted by increasing dissatisfaction with the government's ability and willingness to use development funds effectively. Faced with the choice of withdrawing development assistance to Bangladesh or finding alternative ways to disburse their funds, these agencies decided to experiment with providing funds directly to local NGOs, many of whom had begun to demonstrate their effectiveness in reaching the rural poor with innovative and populist programmes. In certain cases, northern NGOs also played an important role in encouraging their donor agencies to support local NGOs directly. CIDA, for example, began providing funding directly to Proshika in the early 1980s as a result of encouragement by Canadian University Services Overseas (CUSO) who had worked with Proshika for some time. Similarly, GSS's partnership with a Swedish NGO, Diakonia, created the conditions for subsequent access to direct funding from SIDA. Such partnerships between Bangladeshi and northern NGOs gave the former a high profile and some credibility within the development community which was important in underwriting their candidature as recipients of direct funding.

Many donor agencies argued that 'a desire to strengthen civil society' was their main reason for supporting NGOs through direct funding. Before such phrases became fashionable there was a view that working with NGOs might be efficient because the organisations were perceived to be lean and have lower overhead costs. It was assumed that they could therefore maximise the effectiveness of development assistance at low cost. The NGO focus on people rather than infra-structural projects, especially at a time when NGOs were going through a populist phase of building peoples' organisations, was seen as worth being associated with and likely to be popular with constituencies of taxpayers at home.

Resources made available by donor agencies to local NGOs have been drawn from the traditional instruments of bilateral development co-operation. These mechanisms were designed to make available substantial funds for large, state-implemented, infra-structural programmes (e.g. building of roads, dams, hospitals). Resources for Bangladeshi NGOs have been made available in two, quite distinct, forms. The bulk has been in the form of substantial block grants (in excess of US$1 million dollars) to a few selected NGOs to enable them to scale up programmes in health, education and micro-finance.[3] These funds included provisions for core expenses of the NGOs concerned. The size of these grants has increased over time and they now consume the lion's share of funding to the sector. Donor agencies consider that such forms of funding enable lessons learned in the NGO sector about the design and implementation of projects to be applied to comparable programmes initiated by the state. Donor agencies considered that through the use of this instrument they achieved their objective of delivering aid more efficiently and effectively to the grass roots. For their part, the larger NGOs have demonstrated their ability to scale up micro-level projects, a process that has involved some trade-off between effectiveness and efficiency.

The second form of direct funding involved establishing a substantial fund from which resources were made available in the form of large numbers of

---

[3] See funding of Proshika, above n. 2. DFID have funded GSS *circa* US$10m for work in primary education.

small grants to a plethora of smaller NGOs. Funding decisions were made on a project-by-project basis at the discretion of the local office of the donor agency. Typically, discrete projects undertaken by NGOs were those funded, usually with no provisions for meeting core expenses. Frequently, grants were made available on the basis of the priorities and preoccupations of the donor agency, to enable projects to be developed on these themes. This type of funding has enabled donors to develop contacts with a greater number of NGOs than would have been possible within the context of official bilateral co-operation. However, the effectiveness of small NGO grants in terms of efficient aid delivery is less obvious. Both the size and duration of the grant (small and for a fixed period of time) have been major constraints to project effectiveness. The small size of the grant is a clear barrier to the type of economies of scale enjoyed by the larger NGOs. While smaller NGOs may have smaller overhead expenditures, the unit cost of delivering aid per beneficiary is often much higher. Furthermore, the use of fixed-term grants can circumscribe continuity of the project. It is not uncommon for NGOs to suspend work or alter the objectives of a project because of inability to maintain a steady flow of funding from one donor.

Box 2.1: USAID

USAID alone among the donor community has no significant experience with direct funding in Bangladesh. While a total of fifty-seven local NGOs receive USAID funding, this takes place through partner organisations, namely Pathfinder International and the Asia Foundation. Both of these organisations have undergone an extensive vetting process by the US government and have been able to meet the rigid eligibility, reporting and monitoring criteria necessary to receive USAID funds. These organisations are responsible for the identification of suitable projects and local NGOs to be supported. They themselves handle reporting and monitoring. USAID's view is that there are very few local NGOs who possess the managerial skills necessary to work directly with USAID. However, discussions are now under way with some larger NGOs to explore the possibility of initiating a direct funding relationship which may develop into an arrangement where the NGO will act as an intermediary partner for smaller NGOs.

PERSPECTIVES ON DIRECT FUNDING

Once greeted as an important innovation for working with NGOs, the long-term future of direct funding in Bangladesh seems to be in doubt. The emergence of DFID and EU as significant funding agencies has taken place at a time when several smaller donor agencies such as CIDA and NORAD have begun to re-examine their own policies on direct funding. Both NORAD and DANIDA felt that the administrative and managerial costs associated with maintaining a large number of relationships with smaller NGOs may not have been justified by the end-product. Consequently, they have begun to scale back on the number of small NGOs with whom they work. Other donor agencies argue, however, that they have a different set of expectations from the smaller NGOs than from the big ones, and therefore exercise a comparably relaxed set of criteria to maintain accountability with the smaller ones.

One of the main criticisms from within sections of the donor community centres on the sheer size of some of the large NGOs. Two factors seem to be in play. First, the feasibility of continuing to fund the massive programmes run by the well-established NGOs may be in question. As the smaller donors have pointed out, domestic budget constraints have called into question the continued flow of funds for development assistance. Given such changes in the political economy of aid, exasperation has been expressed towards NGOs who continue to expand the scale of their operations at the expense of consolidation. In particular, there has been a perception among some donor agencies that the larger NGOs have been taking the continued flow of donor funds for granted, and that there appears to be an inability or unwillingness on the part of such NGOs to look for alternative sources of funding. Whether these perceptions are valid is debatable: the criticism ignores the real and successful efforts of BRAC and, to a lesser extent, Grameen and Proshika, to consolidate and to become much more financially self-reliant. The alleged increasing bureaucratisation and top-heavy administration of NGOs' central office operations has led several of the smaller donors to question whether the original reasons for funding local NGOs were valid any longer. As a result, several donors have indicated that they will be phasing out their funding relationships with larger NGOs.

Several of the smaller donor agencies have expressed concern about the way in which the better-endowed donor agencies who have previously been unwilling to support NGOs had subsequently become keen to jump onto the NGO bandwagon. There is concern that such donor agencies are beginning to wield a disproportionate amount of influence within donor consortia by virtue of the size of funds they have been able to mobilise. The smaller donor agencies feared that the character of their relationship with partner NGOs has changed and that this has had a negative impact on the quality of work, and believed that there has been failure to learn from past experience. They were concerned by what they perceived as a new 'second tier' of NGOs (including ASA, BURO Tangail and, to a lesser extent, Rangpur-Dinajpur Rural Development Service) being lined up as potential recipients of significant funds to expand the scale of their operations. They believed that this may have been done without sufficient consideration being given to the impact on the sector as a whole.

Box 2.2: Donor Consortia in Bangladesh

A consortium model of funding, whereby all agencies involved co-ordinate funding, has been adopted by a number of NGOs in Bangladesh. NGOs themselves had sought such a strategy with a view to simplifying reporting arrangements. This model of funding has been successful in a number of ways. It has enabled NGOs to reduce paperwork. Donors obtain an overview of all project activities, not just the part that they have funded. It has provided a forum for discussions on the relative advantages of core and project funding. But there are also difficulties that have emerged between members of consortia that reflect the gradual shift in the balance of power within the donor community with regard to the funding of NGOs, especially as a result of the growing influence of DFID and EU. The consortium was once seen as a vehicle for closer co-operation and the development of a genuine partnership between an NGO and its donors, the view of some of the smaller donors and representatives of northern NGOs is that the meetings tend to be preoccupied with discussions on financial accountability and reporting procedures at the expense of reflecting on achievement or progress. The fact that the donor consortium has become the arena for major policy decisions on future interventions to be debated and resolved, has had the unintended effect of shifting the focus of decision-making even further afield.

One important factor that has influenced the way donor agency policies work with NGOs has been changes in the political situation in Bangladesh, particularly the 1991 elections that brought the Bangladesh National Party (BNP) to power in the first free and fair election in over two decades. Donor agencies felt that the new situation was qualitatively different to that which prevailed in the Ershad era. There was a growing view, especially amongst those northern governments with a strong history of state supported welfare and social service systems at home (e.g. Canada, Norway and Sweden), that it was inappropriate to continue supporting structures in parallel with government. NGOs were required, therefore, to explore greater collaboration with government ministries. One donor went as far as to argue that the principal goal (and ultimate measure of the sustainability) of social service programmes should be that they were funded through the domestic budget.

The new mood may become a powerful weapon for a government that would like nothing better than to exert closer control of local NGOs. NGOs are concerned because not all their activities are likely to be supported by the government. Non-service and non-traditional activities such as popular theatre and even some environmental projects run the risk of being deemed inessential. And with few exceptions, NGOs seemed ill-prepared for the type of collaboration being suggested. While there have several examples of government–NGO co-operation, the relationships have been far from ideal.

One major result of these shifts in mood has been the rediscovery of the small NGO. Although the decline in aid budgets has been a force in shifting views (at least in some northern countries), bilateral donors have increasingly been citing many of the traits and characteristics of partnership associated with the relationship between northern and southern NGOs as reasons for exploring closer relationships with small NGOs. This is most evident with CIDA who have already decided to scale back the amount of funding to large NGOs and focus more on small grants administered through their Project Support Unit in their local office.

For DANIDA and SIDA, the question was not so much whether to carry out direct funding or not, but rather over the form that funding should take. SIDA used direct funding only in three countries: India, Sri Lanka and Bangladesh, with the bulk going to Bangladesh. SIDA has been re-evaluating the sectors in which it wishes to continue support, as well as reviewing its policy regarding support to larger NGOs. The character of SIDA's direct funding relationships with NGOs has shifted from one of support for scaling up interventions, towards support for projects which SIDA believes to have greater multiplier effects, and which would strengthen the links between NGOs and the government.

DANIDA have adopted a sectoral and geographical approach to their development funding. Support for the larger NGOs remains an important aspect of Danish development assistance. The agency had been criticised by some of its partners for apparent lack of co-ordination between the implementation of some of the projects it supports. For example, DANIDA had been encouraging RDRS and ASA to expand their operations to the coastal areas of Noakhali and Patuakhali while simultaneously funding a local NGO (the Community Development Centre (CODEC)) that worked in the same regions and of which it had much more intimate local knowledge. There were fears that as a result wastage and duplication may have been associated with competition between NGOs, and resentment could have grown over DANIDA's failure to co-ordinate work.

THE IMPACT OF DIRECT FUNDING

The decision by donor agencies to work more closely with the sector as a whole has had a profound impact on the character of the sector. The most significant change has been that direct funding has led to the creation of a two-tier NGO sector in Bangladesh. The greatest dividends have been reaped by a small handful of NGOs including BRAC, Proshika, GSS and Gonoshystha Kendra (GK) who, between them, account for three-quarters of all funds channelled to the sector. These are the organisations that usually spring to mind when discussing NGOs in Bangladesh, a country with a reputation for having a strong and influential NGO sector. But, direct funding has also contributed to the growth of a large number of smaller NGOs and CBOs working in different parts of the country. The conditions and constraints faced by, and the opportunities and options available to, this section of the NGO community have been very different to those faced by the larger NGOs.

Underlying any discussion about the efficacy of different funding mechanisms is the fundamental question: What is the best way of maximising the impact of the kind of programmes that NGOs undertake? There have been numerous attempts to provide a conceptual framework to this debate (for example see Clark 1991; Howes and Sattar 1992; Wood 1993). The set of distinctions that have most bearing on this study are best summarised by Howes and Sattar who, writing in relation to the policies followed by BRAC, identified three main options for maximising the impact of NGO interventions: *additive strategies*, where impact is achieved through an increase in the size of programme and of the organisation implementing it; *multiplicative strategies*, where impact is achieved through a process of influence, networking, training and legal and policy reforms; and, *diffusive strategies*, where impact is achieved through both informal and spontaneous processes.

Access to substantial funds has been a major factor in enabling and encouraging the better established NGOs to follow an additive strategy for maximising impact enabling NGOs to replicate successful pilot projects on a mass scale. The appeal of this type of approach is enormous for both NGOs and donors alike. As Edwards and Hulme (1992) point out, a commitment to poverty alleviation naturally leads to a desire to reach as many of the poor as possible with a successful project. But in Bangladesh, it seems to have created a culture where the *sole* measure of success is the scale and extent of the replication process. In education, for example, BRAC and GSS have been locked in a fierce competition to open the most schools over the next five years, as if that alone would provide validation to what are commonly acknowledged to be highly innovative and effective approaches to non-formal education. This is a competition that seems to be driven more by a desire to demonstrate capacity to scale up for the sake of scale rather than as part of a strategy to achieve the broader goal of poverty alleviation, or as a means for expanding the range of choices available to the poor.

The emphasis on additive strategies, once seen as the logical means of increasing the impact of NGO interventions, may now be emerging as the Achilles heel of the sector. The trade-offs and compromises that accompany this strategy are considerable, affecting both the nature of the organisation, its values and the impact on the quality of work. At the organisational level, NGOs have had to struggle with problems of an increased hierarchical structure, drawing a distinction between the management of field operations and the management of the organisation. This has increased specialisation and compartmentalisation and perhaps most importantly, established the need to increase the capacity to raise both material and human resources significantly. Increasing proportions of resources have had to be devoted to management of a large and complex organisation, encouraging the emergence of a centralised bureaucracy. Senior managers of the larger NGOs considered that their ability to attract significant funds from the donor agencies was in part due to the fact that they had a substantial organisational infrastructure. At the same time, however, they were having to make major investments to overcome weaknesses in organisational and management capacity.

Ironically, where once NGOs used to claim that their comparative advantage over government programmes was their low overhead costs, simple management and organisational structures, flexibility and responsiveness, today it is their size, complexity and centralised control that makes them attractive to the donors. But these larger NGOs face a potential conundrum: on the one hand, the demands of donors for improved managerial and accountability procedures have steadily increased, with the increasingly large flow of resources to NGOs. They are under constant pressure to invest more in building administrative capabilities. At the same time, donors have begun to raise objections about large institutional structures, over-bureaucratisation and increased centralisation of managerial responsibilities.

SHIFTS IN VALUES AND PHILOSOPHY

One of the unintended impacts of direct funding has been to encourage fundamental shifts in the philosophy and values of the NGO sector. The growing demand for professionalisation, specialisation, goal driven practices, the dominance of quantitative measures of performance and the hegemony of the logical framework, have all contributed to a decline of the spirit of voluntarism which once characterised the sector. Employment with an NGO is perceived as providing the type of security and prestige that was once associated with government service. The category of people seeking to work with NGOs, their motivation and value systems, have begun to change. Not surprisingly, this has had a profound effect on the values that drive the organisation. The people-to-people relationships that were once important features of an NGO have been gradually replaced by an orientation which emphasises procedures, the meeting of specific targets and a culture of self-advancement within the organisation. The achievement of quantitative goals increasingly takes precedence over facilitating social change.

For example, in some credit programmes, field staff have been given specific targets for the number of loans to be made over a given period. This has led field staff to virtually force loans on target group members, even when these are neither needed nor wanted. Some NGOs have begun to penalise field staff if repayment rates are not maintained, a practice that has led to families being forced to sell assets in order to repay loans.

The increasing focus on service delivery has made it difficult for NGOs to move beyond the perception (on the part of beneficiaries) that they are there to provide resources as opposed to creating the conditions where beneficiaries themselves are in a position to demand a more equitable distribution of resources. The role of NGOs as social mobilisers, a role which they held dear in the past, has increasingly been replaced by their new role, created under pressure from the donors, as service providers, with the communities that they serve being transformed into passive recipients of charitable work (in which, of course, they are encouraged to participate). Those organisations such as RDRS who have tried to return to their original role of strengthening people's organisations, find themselves undermined in their work by their NGO competitors, ever eager to take over the role of service providers for projects that attract funds from the donor agencies.

The ability of sections of the NGO community to access bilateral funding directly has been tied to the belief that NGOs possess a significant comparative advantage in the delivery of certain basic services such as primary health care and education and in the provision of credit and other income-generating projects. As a result, those NGOs with well-established programmes in these areas have been able to obtain funding to expand the scale of their operations. The provision of credit has also received a considerable amount of financial support from the donor community in the last five years. In education, both BRAC and GSS have recently received significant grants from DFID and EU to increase the number of schools being run throughout Bangladesh.

Box 2.3: Partners or Contractors?

Whereas the large NGOs may be able to work together with donors as partners, and in certain cases dictate the nature of that relationship, the same is not true for the smaller NGO. In the absence of a charismatic leader such as F. H. Abed or a Mohammed Yunis, the donor is almost always in a dominant position in its dealings with smaller NGOs. Because the funds the donor agencies control frequently represent a major part of the NGO's budget, bilateral donors end up wielding a disproportionate amount of influence over these organisations. One manifestation of this is the emphasis on financial accountability and reporting that accompanies bilateral aid.

One inference from this pattern of funding is that donor agencies have deemed certain activities as being more developmentally relevant than others. Donor agencies appear to be willing to fund those activities which fit with what they perceive to be priorities. The success of the Grameen Bank model precipitated a rush of donor funding for credit activities. Similarly, the increasing emphasis placed by the World Bank on primary education has resulted in an increase in the funds available for such projects. The importance of these types of activity for the future development prospects of Bangladesh is not disputed, but concerns do exist about narrowness of focus. While the provision of alternative sources of credit for the poor has been important in terms of helping to break down dependency on local money-lenders and *mahajans*, major long-term constraints to economic autonomy remain. These include problems in linking this type of intervention with the formal economy. Imperfect markets, lack of market access and inadequate information continue to hamper efforts to initiate and sustain any form of long-term economic growth. Where NGOs have been able to integrate micro-level activities with the markets, it has been through a process of bypassing rather than reforming the system, as in the case of the marketing of Grameen check and silk and handicraft products.

One consequence has been that, whereas there used to be a broad range of interventions carried out within the sector (some more successful than others), there is an increasingly significant degree of homogenisation in the work of NGOs, led principally by the likelihood of attracting funds. Thus, most NGOs now run a combination of programmes as part of an integrated development package consisting of a mixture of health and education projects, and credit and income-generating projects. Even NGOs which, in the past, had vehemently rejected the notion of credit and service-based interventions have found themselves having to respond to the expectations of donors. In the eyes of their target groups, NGOs have also come to be inextricably associated with service delivery.

At the same time, at policy level there is also the very serious question of whether direct funding of the magnitude seen in Bangladesh and the trend towards the removal of primary responsibility for provision of basic social ser-

---

Box 2.4: ASA – from Social Mobilisation to Credit Specialists

One of the most prominent examples of the influence of certain models of development has been the case of the Association for Social Advancement (ASA). Registered formally as an NGO in 1979, ASA pursued a philosophy of using dedicated volunteers to promote village-level groups to struggle for collective social action where ... the focal point of ASA efforts in development is the emergence of a peoples' movement based on awareness and solidarity among the rural peasantry. Funded by a series of northern Church-based organisations, ASA continued to work for social justice through collective action throughout most of the early 1980s. But by the mid-1980s, ASA was already facing some tension between being a membership organisation for the rural poor and being a more formal (intermediary) NGO. However, it was only during the aftermath of the 1987 and 1988 flooding when ASA became involved in providing the type of relief which it had shunned previously that the organisation realised that there is no alternative to credit. At the same time ASA was struggling to redefine its mission statement and the types of programme it would run, and went through a phase of trying to adopt the programmes of other NGOs. By 1991, ASA underwent a process of dramatic transformation from being a peoples' organisation to being a fully-fledged NGO specialising in the delivery of credit. Since then, ASA has emerged as one of the new generation of NGOs challenging established thinking on the provision of credit to the poor. With support from (among others) DANIDA, ASA has been able to increase substantially the scale of its operations, and its partnership with Palli Karma Shahayak Foundation (PKSF) provides it with access to funds made available through the Consultative Group to Assist the Poorest (CGAP). While the experiences represent a process of organic change that is specific to the organisation, the change in approach and the ability to secure funding for this transformation are examples of the profound influence the nature of funding has had on Bangladesh's development terrain.

---

vices from the hands of the state are desirable or whether they have supported privatisation through the back door. The trend towards franchising state services raises serious questions about accountability and the participation of the poor in the decision-making process. As G. D. Wood (1994) points out, at a time when increased emphasis is being placed on the need for accountability and good governance, it is somewhat ironic that donors are tacitly supporting the creation of a system where the relationships between the poor and the state has been largely mediated through NGOs. Given the limited input of beneficiaries to the internal policy-making process of NGOs themselves, treating NGOs as the *de facto* representatives of the poor does not necessarily make it any easier for disenfranchised groups to hold the state responsible or accountable for the provision of basic services.

A related area of concern that follows from this process of homogenisation has been the impact on innovation within the sector. The ability to respond flexibly to the needs of the poor has been one of the main reasons for working with the sector. Over time, this has been transformed into the development and refinement of projects, delivery mechanisms, training and monitoring methods that have been successfully replicated in other countries. Though the degree of innovation within the sector appears to have slowed down in recent years, one noticeable impact of direct funding has been the fact that the locus of innovation has shifted away from the small to the big NGOs. This has largely been because with their access to core funding, the larger NGOs are better able to absorb the much greater risk attached to experimentation and potential failure than a small NGO operating on a limited budget. Although limited funds are sometimes available to smaller NGOs for research and development, the cost of failure will inevitably be much higher. There are few contemporary examples of small NGOs which have developed an innovative and new approach to rural development in the way, for example, that in the past the Grameen Bank did by starting a project with a small Ford Foundation grant.

The fact that direct funding has shifted the arena of innovation towards the larger NGOs is confirmed by the SIDA evaluation which indicated that projects supported through the local bilateral office tended to be of a higher quality and often more relevant than projects supported by Swedish NGOs (Riddell and Bebbington 1995). There were two main reasons for this. First, the local bilateral office had a much better understanding and knowledge of the overall development scene and were able to channel funds to those areas where it might be best used. The scope for linkages between projects supported within the public sector and those supported within the NGO sector was one area in particular where direct funding was seen to have a competitive advantage over indirect funding. In contrast, Swedish NGOs tended, on the whole, to interact with a limited number of local NGOs often affiliated with Church groups who did not

---

Box 2.5: BURO Tangail – another Approach to Credit

BURO Tangail is a small NGO working in the field of credit in Tangail District. It has received direct support for its credit and savings programme from both SIDA and DFID because it proposed an approach that represented a break from the more established Grameen Bank model. The basic aim of its approach is to provide the poor with a range of financial services that are not available through either the formal or the NGO sector. The aim of the project has been to develop a methodology that provides the poor with access to banking services throughout the District. Unlike many other similar programmes, BURO Tangail sees no need to expand its operations beyond the District and are working on a strict timetable for financial independence and sustainability. One major concern facing BURO is the growing competition from other NGOs offering some form of financial services in Tangail. Although many of its members have remained loyal to the programme, some have been attracted by the lower interest rates charged by competitors (BURO's rates are currently 25%) and have left the group. Others have embarked on a process of risk diversification by opting to continue to save with BURO while taking out loans from other NGO programmes. While senior staff at BURO have welcomed the competition and remain confident that they will be able to achieve their goal of working with 100,000 families through 50 branches by the year 2001, there is concern that donors have been providing funds for the expansion of credit programmes into an area where demand is already being met, while the poor in other more remote parts of the country continue to remain dependent on local money-lenders and have not enjoyed any of the benefits of considerable local expertise in the provision of credit.

---

necessarily represent the 'cutting edge' of the NGO sector and, as a result, frequently supported projects that were replications of other well-established interventions.

The one area where small NGOs seem to have been able to maintain their advantage despite the competition from direct funding is that of advocacy and networking. The people-to-people contacts that are a characteristic of partnerships between NGOs is the one area where northern NGOs continue to play an important role. For example, Swallows (the Swedish volunteer sending agency) has begun to focus much of its effort in promoting South–South linkages between their partners in different countries. Thus, at the policy level, attempts have been made to bring Indian and Bangladeshi NGOs together to provide a forum for discussions on environmental issues such as water-sharing that affect both countries. At the level of programming, interventions that have been developed and field tested in one country are being replicated elsewhere in the region and exchange programmes are being facilitated. Certainly northern NGOs have also provided their southern partners with a means of developing partnerships and relationships between communities. These allow for the formation of solidarity groups on issues such as human rights or resistance to the rise of fundamentalist practises that discriminate against women.

The size and the relative importance of the NGO sector has had a major influence on many aspects of life in Bangladesh. From the point of view of direct funding, the most obvious example is in the area of policy-making, especially at the national level. There are, however, differences between the access and influence of the large and small NGOs. Achievements in the areas of health, education and micro-credit have had considerable influence on the work of the government. The establishment of the Integrated Non-Formal Education Project (INFEP) within the Ministry of Education, the resources for rural credit being channelled through the PKSF and, to a lesser extent, the National Drug Policy initiative, are all examples of this influence. Elsewhere, donors have also taken the lead in promoting closer co-operation between the government and NGO sector in agriculture and fisheries. When one looks more closely, however, at the NGOs that have the ability to wield such influence, one tends to see the same few large NGOs: those who have also been the primary beneficiaries of direct funding.

The selective provision of core-funding for only a selected group of larger NGOs while providing only project funding to others suggests that donor agencies may have clear preferences about the types of NGO that they are willing to support in pursuance of their alleged goal of strengthening civil society. One of the most often cited reasons for working with NGOs is that they represent the diversity and pluralism that are seen as one of the keys to sustainable arid democratic growth. Support to the NGO sector is seen as complementary to the emphasis being placed on the importance of governance.

For years, ADAB has endeavoured to provide a forum for smaller NGOs to be heard. It has also been concerned with mediating and co-ordinating activities within the NGO sector. ADAB has yet, however, to gain acceptance as the representative of the NGO community, especially by the larger NGOs. Like larger NGOs elsewhere, those in Bangladesh do not feel the same concern to become members, or have the protection, of an umbrella organisation. With their range of personal contacts, their international profiles, their access to and support from the donor community and their personal friendships with officials in the state, the large NGOs feel quite secure about making representations of their own interests. Furthermore, where there is a sense that the government

Box 2.6: The Role of ADAB in the Non-co-operation Movement

The 1995–6 non-co-operation movement that resulted in the resignation of the government provides an interesting example of the lack of a unified voice within the NGO community. Mindful, perhaps, of criticism of the NGO community's failure in 1991 to participate fully in the movement that overthrew the Ershad government, NGOs played a prominent role. Under the leadership of Kazi Farooq Ahmed (Chief Executive of Proshika), ADAB joined the movement for the establishment of a caretaker government along with representatives of the business community. This represented the coming together of different sections of civil society to force a resolution of the impasse between the political parties that had effectively paralysed normal life in Bangladesh for over two years. Prior to its capitulation and resignation, Ershad's government launched a series of attacks on ADAB and its chairperson. It questioned the legitimacy of foreign-funded organisations indulging in party politics. It went on to ridicule ADAB as representing only a handful of marginal NGOs and claimed that the position taken by ADAB in calling for a caretaker government had not been endorsed by 'proper' NGOs such as BRAC. This attempt to divide the NGOs was repudiated in a series of advertisements taken out by BRAC in the local press, but the point about questioning ADAB's authority and claims of representation had been made. The repercussions remain to be seen, but it became apparent that ADAB's rank-and-file membership had not been properly consulted prior to the decision to come out in favour of the non-co-operation movement. This was clearly an error and served to illustrate an institutional weakness of the network. More surprising, however, was the reaction of many members of the donor community, including certain northern NGOs (who were also members of ADAB). Almost without exception the feeling was that ADAB (in particular its chairperson) had somehow acted beyond the terms of its brief and that NGOs should not have assumed a position on the political crisis. Therein lay a contradiction. On the one hand these same institutions emphasise the importance of good governance and the involvement of NGOs as part of civil society. On the other, there were protestations when NGOs sought to involve themselves in activities which would generally be termed as advocacy. If the message coming out of the donor community is that advocacy puts NGOs into an awkward position with the government and should therefore be avoided, then the role of the NGO is more emphatically than ever being reduced to that of service deliverers. Were NGOs to accept this, it would only serve to further weaken their position with regard to the rest of civil society.

Box 2.7: The Bangladesh Environmental Lawyers Association (BELA)

BELA registered itself as an NGO in 1992. Originally established to oppose the World Bank's Flood Action Plan, BELA has subsequently established a niche for itself within the NGO community. BELA has been able to forge important working relationships with operational NGOs and has provided training on environmental law. It is an active member of the coalition of environmental NGOs. BELA initially funded itself by accepting consultancies, the lawyers working on a *pro bono* basis. More recently, however, BELA has been funded by both the Ford Foundation and the Aga Khan Foundation, as well as by the Netherlands Organisation for International Development Co-operation (NOVIB) and CIDA (through the Canada Fund). BELA is an example of the type of high returns from a small investment that many donors are seeking.

---

may have reservations about umbrella organisations, larger NGOs may prefer to keep them at arm's length lest their image and their own substantial interests are marred by association. In contrast, the smaller NGOs, and especially those without offices in the capital city, are acutely aware of their vulnerability to the vagaries of local officials, and benefit considerably from the solidarity and supportive environment provided by alliances with other NGOs. Despite the alleged desire to help strengthen civil society, they have provided little support to ADAB that would enable it to assume its responsibilities in representing the interests of the NGO sector.

The availability of direct funding in Bangladesh has had a contradictory impact on the development of civil society. The support has helped nurture a degree of plurality within the sector. But a strong development NGO sector is not necessarily synonymous with a strong civil society. Critics of the sector have argued that development NGOs have grown at the expense of other civil society organisations. Others have accused development NGOs of luring away their workers with the promise of better salaries and more stable employment provided by access to foreign funds. Given the somewhat uncomfortable relationship between development NGOs and other civil society actors, some have questioned whether the way in which the donor agencies have sought to strengthen development NGOs at the expense of other civil society actors may be part of an implicit or explicit aim of recreating a civil society in the South that resembles that in the North, regardless of whether or not the socio-economic and cultural conditions would lend themselves to that configuration.

THE EFFECT OF DECLINING AID BUDGETS

The threat of declining aid transfers to Bangladesh and elsewhere has sparked off a scramble within the sector over a shrinking pool of resources. This process of forced rationalisation is working in favour of the larger well-established NGOs. With an emphasis on consolidation, many of the smaller NGOs have found it difficult to maintain their individual identities and autonomy in the face of competition from better resourced NGOs. Even relatively well-known NGOs, such as RDRS and Saptagram have found it difficult to access direct funding. Saptagram, for example, was able to access direct bilateral funding (in this case from SIDA) only after the adoption of a very specific form of focus on Women in Development (WID) and the creation of special pools of resources to support the work of women's organisations.

In both cases, attempts to address sustainability issues by gradually phasing out direct involvement in service delivery have been threatened by the expansion of a better resourced NGO into their working areas. While this might be seen as an example of healthy competition within the sector, it is also evidence of the culture of dependence and patron–client relationships that has largely been unchanged by the expansion of the NGO sector. Thus RDRS's attempts to phase out of direct involvement with about 5,000 groups and to concentrate on strengthening the peoples' organisation capacity to meet the needs of their members by providing training and other inputs have been hindered by the fact that BRAC and ASA have recently begun work in the Rangpur-Dinajpur areas. Both these organisations have, ironically, ended up working with erstwhile members of RDRS's target group thereby undermining efforts to gradually make the peoples' organisation self-reliant.

Nevertheless, there has been a realisation that it is unlikely that the current levels of funding for NGOs will be maintained in the foreseeable future. This has brought into sharper relief some of the major contradictions running through the sector. Different NGOs have responded to the need for greater consolidation in different ways. BRAC, for example, has become increasingly mindful of the impact that it has on the work of other (especially smaller) NGOs and is exploring several different options. The first of these relates to internal choices about the future direction of both the Rural Development Programme (RDP) and the Rural Credit Programme (RCP) where the limitations of the additive strategy of growth are now beginning to make themselves evident. While BRAC is making attempts to diversify its sources of funding and is apparently able to generate up to 40% of its own budget, it is unlikely that it will be able to maintain this rate of expansion without compromising the integrity of its programmes. Thus, we have seen a re-emergence of concerns about the need to focus on quality rather than low unit costs so that BRAC can continue to maintain a comparative advantage relative to other NGOs. Focus on the quality of interventions has led to BRAC working more closely with smaller NGOs and CBOs who wish to replicate BRAC programmes, especially in health and education. BRAC now works with around 137 partner NGOs in the area of non-formal education and has assumed responsibility for material development, training and monitoring, while leaving actual implementation to the smaller partner NGOs. BRAC has also been working more closely with government counterparts to help to strengthen the capacity of local officials and to facilitate qualitative change in the formal government sector.

Elsewhere, NGOs such as Proshika and GSS have opted for a more active role in national level advocacy. Proshika has recently established an Institute for Development Policy, Analysis and Advocacy (IDPAA). It hopes to initiate, in combination with international and national bodies, work on policies that will address the needs of the poor. Increasingly, realisation seems to grow throughout the sector that the impact of micro-level successes will continue to be limited unless a way is found of initiating changes at the meso and macro levels of society. Similarly, GSS has also begun to work more closely with other NGOs in the area of non-formal education and legal rights and have provided important logistical and technical support to other NGOs in the field. It is too early to predict what impact IDPAA, and other attempts for an increased NGO involvement in advocacy issues, will have on the broader policy environment. The movement towards multiplicative and diffuse strategies of increasing impact may perhaps be an indication that some of the problematic issues surrounding the use of direct funding might still be overcome.

CONCLUSION

The key point to emerge from this case study is the need for donors and NGOs alike to understand better the gains and losses that are associated with direct funding. If one looks at the history of the mechanism, it is apparent that the driving force behind direct funding was a desire to increase the quantity of aid money available to the sector. However, it is the quality of aid which is the key variable in determining whether NGOs lose or increase their effectiveness as a result of a direct funding relationship with bilateral donors.

In the case of Bangladesh, and with the benefit of hindsight, one can see that the importance of the distinction between quantity and quality of aid has not been fully appreciated. Partly this has to do with the nature of the sector and its relationships with other civil society actors at the time when direct funding emerged as a key policy tool in the donor community. What concerns did exist with regard to direct funding had to do with the impact it would have on individual NGOs. The issue of the broader impact on the development of the sector as a whole did not feature very prominently in the discussions on the relative merits and demerits of the system.

When direct funding was first proposed, it was greeted as an important innovation in development assistance. It was a reflection of the prevailing wisdom of the time that considered it important to attempt to scale up micro-level projects which in turn would lead to progress in the struggle for poverty alleviation. The fact that the major NGOs have been able successfully to scale up interventions in health, education and micro-finance would appear to justify that belief. During the study, the issue of NGOs becoming bureaucratised and losing their comparative advantage has been raised in several contexts. However, while concerns about these potential impacts continue to exist and will undoubtedly re-emerge in other countries, several points need to be kept in mind. Part of the success of many NGO programmes has been the emphasis on monitoring and supervision. What NGOs have been able to demonstrate is that it is possible to develop high-quality interventions and to sustain that quality if the time and resources exist to maintain the system. The flip side of this is the fact that as programmes are taken to scale and added to, there will inevitably be an increased degree of bureaucratisation. It is not possible for an NGO such as BRAC to accommodate an annual budget in excess of US$50 million (1997), while still remaining decentralised and flexible to the extent that it had been when the scale of operation was restricted to a few villages. Having said that, choices remain for both donors and NGOs alike.

From the point of view of NGOs, the need to devolve decision-making to field level cannot be overstated. One of the major problems facing the larger NGOs is the degree to which this is possible given the way in which programmes have developed. But as Rutherford (1995) points out in relation to ASA, decentralisation is possible without necessarily sacrificing transparency and accountability. A related point is the lack of a formalised procedure for beneficiaries to input into the decision-making processes of the NGO within the context of scaling up.

From the point of donors, there is a need to specify the thinking behind the desire to fund NGOs directly, to be explicit about the expectations that accompany these decisions, and to show a willingness to move beyond an over-emphasis on formal reporting mechanisms. It is important to realise that direct funding that is designed to increase the efficient use and delivery of aid will lead to the establishment of procedures and mechanisms that will inevitably make NGOs more top-heavy and centrally guided. If on the other hand, the aim is to support NGOs as part of a genuine desire to strengthen civil society, allowances will have to be made to enable NGOs to maintain their comparative advantage in terms of flexibility and responsiveness.

What of the value of additive, as opposed to other, strategies? If the belief is that impact is determined by scale alone, then the objections raised by donors about over-bureaucratisation are clearly disingenuous. One implication of this is that the sector will have to undergo considerable rationalisation if circumstances do not change: the larger NGOs are better placed to undergo the transformation into intermediary organisations and assuming the type of role that was once filled by northern NGOs. One can also anticipate a degree of rationalisation in terms of the types of programme that will continue to be funded, and within that context increased sectoral specialisation is likely.

On the one hand, it could be that this specialisation will yield significant efficiency gains and lead to the promotion of greater choice among NGO beneficiaries. At the same time, however, it could also lead to a significant change in the character of the sector with NGOs taking on more of the traits of private-sector business organisations, moving away from the values of voluntarism and altruism that have been at the heart of the NGO movement. One can already see a move in this direction. BRAC, and to a lesser extent Proshika, have developed a corporate attitude and philosophy that is similar to that found in the private sector, with the emphasis being placed on professionalism and procedures. Fowler's contention that the introduction of multiple accountabilities and changing sets of norms and values may well lead to NGOs losing their civicness and democratising potential as a result of closer involvement with official agencies remains a major source of concern (Fowler 1994). But at the same time, it could also help to dispel some of the myths about NGOs.

One could argue that a by-product of the increase in resources available to NGOs has been the creation of unreasonable expectations. NGOs are no different from any other type of organisation working in the field of development and they cannot be expected to shoulder the burden of rural development any more than government agencies or parastatals have had to in the past. NGOs are clearly an important part of the solution, but as Fowler (1996) points out, the resources to promote closer inter-NGO co-operation as well as closer co-operation with other civil society actors and the government are essential if the quality of NGO interventions is not going to end up being compromised by institutional constraints. This is particularly true at the grass-roots level where relationships with local officials and groups tend to be overshadowed by a general external orientation towards the centre. NGOs have not been afraid to use their influence with donors and senior government officials to resolve problems at the local level, which only seems to emphasise divisions and animosities. But if the civic and democratic character of the NGO sector is to be preserved and strengthened, donor agencies are going to have to maintain a much lower profile and will have to allow NGOs to forge independent links with local groups and organisations. Some of these may lead to partnerships which donors find problematic, but this is the price they must pay.

There can be little doubt that direct funding has fundamentally altered the nature of the NGO sector in Bangladesh and the nature of its relationships with other civil society actors – in some cases for the better and in other cases not. The challenge for both donors and NGOs alike is to move away from a simple analysis of positive and negative impacts of this trend. The most important lesson to be learned is the need to clearly specify the aims and objectives for funding NGOs. To do so there is a need to move beyond a simple focus on the individual recipient NGO to try to understand some of the broader consequences that accompany a significant transfer of resources through the sector. This has been the missing element in the case of Bangladesh. Thus, we have a situation where NGOs are caught between being partners and contractors. On the one hand, donors clearly would like to see their relationships with NGOs being based on a partnership of equals. But too often the practical expectations and mechanisms used have been those of contracting. Given the diversity of the sector, there is no reason to suppose that a dual policy cannot be maintained. Certain NGOs clearly see themselves and their role as being service deliverers while others do not. An enlightened donor policy to the NGO sector would be to allow the space for both types of NGO and relationships to co-exist within the broader umbrella of a strong sector that is both representative and effective as a voice for NGOs.

While the benefits from direct funding remain high, so do the costs, and the challenge is to maintain an awareness of this and to improve understanding of where and how NGOs fit into the broader policy mix. In the case of Bangladesh, certain allowances can be made because of the fact that when it began, direct funding represented a new way of working with NGOs, and mistakes and unforeseen consequences were to some extent inevitable. The same is not true for other countries, and the lesson from Bangladesh is that direct funding can have a very profound impact on the shape and values of the sector.

Chapter 3

Peru: 'The Death of Development as Social Transformation'

CHANGES IN THE FUNDING ENVIRONMENT

The Peruvian economy was once considered to be one of the most promising in Latin America owing to the wealth of its natural resources. However, extensive government intervention in pricing, interest rates, credit allocation and labour markets, as well as dictatorial policies led to political crises and economic decline in the 1980s. There have been large-scale migrations from rural to urban areas, with negative economic and social repercussions. During the 1980s, terrorist activities resulted in further urban migration and a marked reduction of agricultural and industrial productivity. Under the Garcia administration (1985–90), Peru underwent one of the deepest and most rapid examples of economic deterioration experienced by any country in peacetime this century: per capita consumption by the poorest 20% of the population, for example, declined by 60%. By 1990, these imbalances had contributed to hyperinflation, deep recession, massive levels of foreign debt and a marked decline in living standards.

After Alberto Fujimori's election in 1990, an economic reform programme (supported by the World Bank, IMF and IDB) was instituted that succeeded in reducing inflation from an annual average of 7,600% in 1990 to 24% in 1994, the lowest rate for seventeen years. Peru had taken a major step towards reintegration into the international financial community by clearing its debts with the IMF and the World Bank. As a result, flows of funds from these institutions were reinstituted. The improved political and economic conditions resulted in increased confidence of private international investors, and foreign investment rose from negative levels pre-1992 to US$2,326 million in 1994.

Despite these dramatic improvements, exchange rates have remained high, the flow of public revenue was uncertain, real interest rates remained high and debts to the commercial banks continued to be substantial. The impact of terrorism and guerrilla warfare on the economy and social situation has been reduced since the capture of the leaders of Shining Path, but coca production and the drug trade continued to flourish. By 1996, the proportion of people described as living in extreme poverty had declined from 25% to 16%. Nevertheless, about 11 million people lived below the poverty line with insufficient food, inadequate housing, education and sanitation, and in poor health.

Both the World Bank and Inter-American Development Bank (IDB) have supplied substantial funds for the privatisation of state firms, restructuring of public administration, reconstruction of the national road network, reform of the public education and health systems, rural electrification and urban and rural sanitation. Assistance for budget/balance-of-payment programmes associated with economic structural adjustment programmes has increased. The area that has benefited most since 1992 is economic management, which has received more than half the total resources. Contributions towards food aid also rose, while the volume directed to other areas, such as environmental protection and agriculture, declined.

DONOR AGENCY FUNDING TO THE NGO SECTOR

While international finance institutions have begun to look more favourably at Peru, there has nevertheless been an overall reduction in the total aid budget available during the 1990s. Peru remains one of the leading recipients of aid in Latin America, however, the continent receives less than 10% of annual international disbursements of aid. In 1992, 68% of aid funds to Peru were provided from bilateral sources (principally Japan, USA, Italy, Canada, the Netherlands and Spain), while multilateral organisations supplied 27%. Only 5% came from northern NGOs (Valderrama 1997). Nevertheless, the volume of funds disbursed to the NGO sector in Peru has grown considerably since the early 1990s. The 1990s have been characterised by a growing enthusiasm for NGOs on the part of multilateral and bilateral agencies, with political pressure being exerted on the government also to channel funds to NGOs.

There were various reasons why official agencies directed an increasing proportion of their funds to the NGO sector. Some agencies appeared to regard NGOs as being able to provide effective delivery of specific services. Others saw funding them as a way of supporting democratic processes and strengthening civil society by encouraging greater pluralism in societies dominated by autocratic regimes and single party states. It was also seen by some agencies as a means of increasing their political influence in Peru, and as a way of indirectly influencing government policies and procedures.

USAID: Before the mid-1980s, USAID did not directly fund any NGO work in Peru, focusing its attention on infrastructural development instead. Since then, however, its NGO programme has grown considerably. USAID decided to support the NGO sector, apparently, because of its desire to support democracy and stability, and as part of its strategy against both the influence of Shining Path, and the effects of the growing drug industry. By 1996 USAID had become the largest source of funds for NGOs in Peru, even though its total aid disbursement to Peru had declined from a high of US$130 million a year in 1995 to an annual projection of US$90 million for the five-year period from 1997. USAID funds were targeted primarily for programmes related to building democracy (including narcotics education and private sector institutional reform), micro-enterprise and income-generating projects (including an NGO support programme), food security, health (including commercial family planning) and environmental and natural resource management.

The sizeable grants that USAID provided (for example, Manuela Ramos received grants of between US$17 and US$20 million) have created substantial difficulties for NGOs who do not necessarily have the infrastructure for managing either large budgets or the considerable paperwork associated with USAID procedures for project management. In some cases, USAID had put their own staff into these agencies to revise accounting, procurement and other policies and procedures to ensure they suited USAID's own requirements. The high level of technical and financial requirements imposed by USAID has created difficulties for NGOs, especially as it has led to an increase in overhead costs, making them less competitive when seeking funds elsewhere. Many NGOs have expressed fears about the extent of dependency created by grants received from USAID.

Funding from USAID has frequently been provided under a system of competitive tendering. USAID identifies a project or programme which it deems is required. NGOs are then asked to demonstrate their capacity to implement the USAID defined programme. This approach has created two sets of problems for local NGOs. First, few have the experience to prepare the types of proposal that are required to compete successfully for tenders. Inevitably, US organisations such as PACT and CARE, with their greater knowledge and experience of the norms and mores of USAID, have frequently been able to compete successfully against local NGOs. Secondly, the approach has been viewed as reducing the work of NGOs to being subcontractors carrying out a programme of work defined by the official agency instead of by local organisations or the communities with whom they work. Both what is to be delivered and how it is to be done is usually determined by USAID according to its own priorities and values, while the NGO is left to be a subcontractor.

CIDA: Peru has for many years been the most significant recipient of Canadian official assistance in Latin America. The Canadian embassy administered a variety of projects in Peru, including economic support programmes that supplied Canadian mining, petroleum and telecommunications equipment to Peru. This programme produced counterpart funds (see below) to the value of approximately US$10 million per annum and which has been used to support various initiatives locally including assistance to an economic research consortium, local universities and NGO research centres. CIDA channelled a significant proportion of funds for the NGO sector through counterpart funds, and a sizeable proportion of CIDA's support is provided to Canadian NGOs operational in Peru. In 1996, CIDA began the process of reviewing its policy for support for government programmes with a view to reinstating Canadian support to the government.

DFID and the British Council: The British Department for International Development (DFID) (formerly ODA) has had relatively little involvement with NGOs in Peru. Most of DFID's programme has been administered through the British Council (which has been present in Peru for many years providing English-language teaching and cultural activities). DFID's Technical Co-operation Officer was based at the British Council. British interests have been focused principally in health, supporting government based health care and family planning services. DFID has had no direct involvement with local NGOs, channelling most of their funds for the sector through British NGOs such as CARE, Marie Stopes International, ITDG and Oxfam UKI.

Counterpart funds: A sizeable and growing proportion of funds made available to the NGO sector in Peru has been sourced in counterpart funds. Peru's first experience of counterpart funds was with the creation of the Peru–Canada General Counterpart Fund (PCGCF) in 1989. The system was introduced after the Garcia government (1985–90) decided unilaterally to reduce the servicing of Peru's external debt to 10% of the value of exports. In retribution, many commercial banks and government lending agencies cut all operations with Peru. However, CIDA was reluctant to reduce its programme in Peru and so decided to use a mechanism that it had previously employed in other countries. The mechanism enabled CIDA to accumulate a fund in local currency in Peru in the following manner: where local companies or the government had placed orders for goods from Canada, CIDA arranged to pay the Canadian supplier directly in Canadian currency while the purchaser paid CIDA for the goods in local currency. This enabled CIDA to accumulate a substantial fund in local currency which it then used to make grants, often to the NGO sector in Peru. A number of Canadian NGOs, such as World University Service of Canada (WUSC), CUSO and CanSave also obtained grants from this fund. Disbursements to the value of approximately US$44 million were made between 1989 and 1994, and in 1996 it was expected that future annual disbursements would be about US$10 million per year. PCGCF has also managed a credit fund presently valued at US$12 million. Through the use of counterpart funds, CIDA has supported some 130 agencies, including local NGOs, community-based organisations and local government projects, with the majority being disbursed for rural programmes, credit and economic and productive projects. The average size of a grant was US$300,000 for up to three years in 1995.

The success of the Canadian experience prompted the creation of similar instruments by others, including the EU, Switzerland and Japan. The EU instrument was based on the monetisation of food aid, the Swiss Fund on a debt swap scheme and the Japanese Fund from the sale of agricultural equipment. The budgets have ranged between US$7.5 and 14 million per annum. Over the last three years the EU, Switzerland and Japan have disbursed US$30 million a year, mostly for supporting projects associated with mitigating the effects of economic structural adjustment programmes, usually directed towards the same geographic locations.

To reduce the costs of administration of the fund, aid agencies established minimum grant levels. In some cases there have been substantial grants made of sums far greater than most NGOs had experience of managing. The average size of grants in 1995 was US$307,000, disbursed over a period of three years. Many NGOs have experienced difficulties managing such sizeable funds because of their weak institutional capacities and because of the complex reporting procedures that the donors imposed. The aid agencies have frequently sought, therefore, to create, or encourage, the formation of consortia of NGOs charged with the responsibility of managing the funds. This experience has not, however, been entirely successful. There have been several NGO consortia formed. Some, such as Coordindora Interinstitucinal para a Desarrollo Rural de Ayacucho (CIDRA), were created independently by NGOs themselves. However, most were established by donor agencies. The principal supporter of consortia, the Canadians, did not make an entirely positive assessment of the virtues of consortia, and became disenchanted and sceptical about the value of consortia for managing funds. They expressed the view that such virtual organisations would be better off focusing on co-ordination, dissemination of information and promotion of discussion on regional development, rather than being involved with project planning or implementation.

Many local NGOs have been critical about the requirements of donor agencies administering counterpart funds. They felt too great a pressure to comply with procedures set by the donors. They believed that donors were more concerned about ensuring formal consistency with the donor's own policies and strategies, having logical frameworks and operational plans set up to their specific requirements and other such formalities, than with what the project sought to achieve, the methodologies used and importance of the project for the beneficiaries. In sum, many NGOs felt that they were being required to do the donor's bidding at the expense of serving the needs of the poor. In order to fulfil the stringent formal requirements set by the donor, many NGOs resorted to hiring consultants to write proposals for them. The unfortunate consequence of this was, in many cases, that the aid agencies believed the NGOs to have a greater capacity to manage the proposed project than was in fact the case.

The vast amounts of funds made available through counterpart funds have created a number of problems in the NGO sector. In many cases, the availability of such funds has acted as a stimulus to the formation of organisations whose primary purpose has been to gain access to the funds. For example, for many years there have been very few NGOs in Hauncavelica: but since counterpart funds began to flow, huge numbers of NGOs have been established with the sole purpose of accessing these funds. The availability of the counterpart funds has had a significant impact on the growth of the number of NGOs in several provincial capitals. Never before has there been such an important supply of development funding for these regions that can be accessed by local NGOs. The pattern in the past had always been one of a handful of big Lima NGOs receiving most of the (private donor) funding, in several cases opening up projects in poor areas. With the counterpart funds this panorama has changed radically and small, local NGOs have received funds that largely exceed the amounts they had had the occasion to manage before. Furthermore, a number of northern NGOs who have faced declining incomes at home had begun to compete with local NGOs for access to counterpart funds with some success, creating resentment amongst some local NGOs.

Increasingly, a number of aid agencies have encouraged the monetisation of food aid, the funds from which are then used, like the counterpart funds, to support local projects. Peru has for many years been a recipient of food aid (primarily from the USA and EU), with the volume rising during the 1990s. According to INTERFAIS, Peru received 414,000 tons of food in 1993, of which 58% was sold through the Associacion Nacional de Industrias at commercial rates.

FONCODES: The Fondo Nacional de Compensacion y Desarrollo Social was created by the Peruvian government in 1991 in co-operation with multilateral organisations as a temporary autonomous agency. Modelled on similar initiatives in Bolivia, its underlying rationale was to provide funding for projects to mitigate the negative social impact of structural adjustment programmes. Until 1993, most of FOCONDES' resources came from the Treasury with only 2% contributed by donors. Since 1994, however, a significant share of its resources (35% in 1994 and 45% in 1995) has come from development banks. The World Bank and IDB have also provided loans for the programme. By the end of the first quarter of 1996, FOCONDES had funded 18,000 projects valued at approximately US$600 million. Funding has been provided for projects concerned with the supply of services or the building of infrastructures for health and education, civil works on roads and energy, and support to foster small-scale productive activities in agriculture, fisheries and commerce.

FONCODES' philosophy has been to support demand-driven projects, so that the beneficiaries participate in the management of their own development. This is thought to ensure sustainability of the projects and stimulate the organisation of the population for future endeavours. Proposals can be submitted to FONCODES by any social group or institution that represents an organised community. Funds have been channelled through various organisations including peasant communities, NGOs and local governments. FONCODES funding has mostly been in the form of grants, although the fund also finances credits for small productive projects. Funds have been allocated according to 'poverty maps' designed by FONCODES on the basis of a set of indicators which includes chronic malnutrition, illiteracy, unemployment and lack of access to basic services. The poorest areas receive the highest priority. Its executive committee normally assigns a promoter with whom they jointly design the project.

There has been much concern amongst NGOs that FONCODES has not acknowledged the experience the sector has accumulated over the past twenty-five years. They believe that FONCODES repeatedly commits all the classic 'do nots' of development. For example, the construction of schools has frequently been undertaken without any consideration of human resource requirements or of how recurrent budget expenses will be met. In the majority of cases analyses of the needs of the community have been formulated by outsiders, despite claims that the projects are demand driven by the community.

FONCODES' regulations dictate that all projects should be assigned external inspectors. Such inspectors are paid a fee by FONCODES. The system has been widely abused as a means of job creation. In the case of Ayacucho, for example, the operation of FONCODES has been the primary incentive for the establishment of a large number of NGOs that were in reality only private subcontractors who were entirely dependent on funds from FONCODES, and who had adopted the legal form of an NGO in order to be eligible to be considered as inspectors.

NGOS IN PERU

Until the 1960s there were virtually no development NGOs in Peru, although there were numerous membership organisations such as trade unions, peasant organisations and political parties. Charitable activities and voluntary work were undertaken largely by church organisations.

The NGO sector (as we know it today) began to emerge in Peru after the victory of Belaunde's Popular Action Party in 1962. Belaunde initiated a programme (modelled on the US Peace Corps) known as Popular Co-operation involving the mobilisation of the voluntary efforts of a broad section of society, especially the youth. This initiative prompted the establishment of a number of NGOs who, experiencing a growing disenchantment with government policies, soon began seeking alternative sources of funds and support. By 1997 there were more than 700 NGOs, comprising an extremely diverse group of organisations, registered with the Ministry of the Presidency's Secretariat for International Technical Co-operation (SECTI).

There have been, essentially, three phases in the development of NGOs in Peru. The first-generation NGOs, largely emerging in the late 1960s and early 1970s, were originally founded to promote grass-roots, or people's organisations. They saw their role as social mobilisers and believed that development was about social transformation. Strongly influenced by Paulo Freire's writings on popular participation and conscientisation, they shared common views about the need for developing community and peasants' organisations as a basis for social and political change. From an early period, many of these NGOs established links and close working relationships with northern NGOs. Many of the individuals involved in the first-generation NGOs were to become leading intellectuals in the emerging field of development, often providing a radical perspective. Their work occasionally led to confrontations with the state, and many suffered in subsequent periods of repression.

The second-generation NGOs were founded during the later 1980s and early 1990s, coinciding with the emergence of neo-liberal ideologies internationally. Partly as a consequence of the experiences of repression and civil war, and partly due to their social background, these NGOs had, from the beginning, an approach to development that was more technical than ideological. They were, generally, concerned less with political or social ideals about grass-roots organisations, and focused more on engaging their professional expertise in undertaking projects concerned with employment generation, technological solutions, small enterprise development, agricultural production and the provision of services such as health care, family planning, vaccinations and child nutrition. They were also less concerned about dealing with injustices, although they have become increasingly involved in helping internally displaced populations. The emergence of the second-generation NGOs was strongly associated with the growth in the availability of funding from both bilateral and multilateral agencies.

A third generation emerged in the early 1990s. The majority established themselves as non-profit associations in order to access funds that were being made available for service provision in poor areas as part of the policy seeking to mitigate the social impact of structural adjustment programmes. The vast majority of these newly formed NGOs are not strictly organisations, but rather temporary formations created to access funds, as contractors, from FON-CODES. Most of them are said to be run by a protector who provides a loose umbrella or front for a series of unconnected projects. The number of such organisations has continued to rise.

THE IMPACT OF DIRECT FUNDING

The initial growth of Peruvian NGOs owed much to the solidarity and financial support provided by northern NGOs in the 1970s. From supporting short-term projects, the northern NGOs became increasingly involved in providing institutional support and core-funding that provided some degree of flexibility in the kinds of operation that Peruvian NGOs could initiate. Consequently, there was a great deal of creativity and development of new methodologies that were, much later, to have a major influence on programmes initiated by other development agencies, including government. Peruvian and northern NGOs confronted each other as equals, with a shared view of the world and of the social changes that they wished to wring through the projects in which they were involved. Northern NGOs saw their work as being an expression of solidarity rather than merely charitable or developmental support.

In the 1990s, however, there were significant changes in the nature of the relationship between Peruvian and northern NGOs. The changes were associated with a number of factors: the decline in the resources available to NGOs in the North, both from official sources and from public donations; the dramatic growth in the volume of funds available to the NGO sector in Peru; the ideological shifts that occurred in association with the rise of the New Right in the USA and Europe; and the rise in the culture of professionalism of NGOs, as part of the professionalisation of development itself.

From the point of view of Peruvian NGOs, two main features characterised the changes. First, northern NGOs began to behave increasingly like the official aid agencies. They were demanding reporting formats, accountability structures, regulations and procedures that were little different to those demanded by the official aid agencies. Northern NGOs had themselves come under increasing pressure from the official agencies to comply with ever stricter regulations, formalities and reporting procedures. Under such circumstances they had little choice but to pass on the same conditions to their local partners. 'The spread of direct funding is not a cause of concern for us', claimed one NGO leader, '[but] the northern NGOs add an expensive and often inefficient bureaucratic layer to the co-operation relationship and we are better off in direct funding relationships with government agencies.' Not surprisingly, this has led to some souring of relationships, with local NGOs echoing the view that they would prefer money to interference, support rather than second-hand rules and regulations passed on from northern governmental donors (Smillie and Helmich 1993).

[The] upheaval for northern NGOs has meant that they have gone back to the concept of financial management that involves allocating resources for specific activities. Discussion no longer centres on objectives, but on project indicators and operational monitoring. This is a result of a number of developments: surging neo-liberalism and cutbacks has made public opinion more critical of the effectiveness of co-operation, which leads to streamlining the imposition of controls by official donors, which in turn, puts pressure on northern NGOs who then apply this zeal for auditing on to their Peruvian partners, which leads to increased control and pragmatism. (Valderrama 1997)

Despite such expressions of Angst, many local NGOs have often found that they needed to forge alliances with northern NGOs in their dealings with external funding agencies. Some organisations have continued to receive small but significant financial support from northern NGOs that has enabled them to maintain a degree of independence that would otherwise have been difficult, especially for funding of activities directed at reconstructing the social tissues of society such as local grass-roots organisations and democratic and human rights concerns. But such kinds of support have become increasingly rare.

Secondly, there has been growing concern among Peruvian NGOs that northern NGOs have become competitors for funds in the Peruvian development market. As access to funds in the North has become more difficult, and as more funds have become available in Peru for the NGO sector, many northern NGOs had decided to engage in local fund-raising in direct competition with local NGOs. Several northern NGOs arranged to register their Peruvian outpost office as indigenous Peruvian NGOs to be eligible to apply for locally available funds such as counterpart funds or those from FONCODES. The result has been that northern NGOs have changed from collaborators and partners to competitors against Peruvian NGOs for the same source of funds.

Such northern NGOs confront local NGOs in a market-place of unequal opportunities. The northern NGOs have long experience of the procedures and requirements of international donor agencies, particularly the official agencies of their home countries. Also, as a constituent part of the donor community, northern NGOs have a substantial network of personal contacts, and influence in that community. In addition, they have access to considerable amounts of technical expertise and resources from their headquarters, and operate with the comfort and assurance that, failing a successful bid, their costs will be guaranteed by their home office. Very few local NGOs can compete successfully against such opponents. Official aid agencies inevitably feel that they can have greater confidence in disbursing funds to a brand name that is recognisable than to unknown local institutions.

The experiences of the Peru office of the UK-based ITDG was a case in point. ITDG started work in Peru in 1987. Its operations were at one time entirely funded by its UK headquarters. Following the developments in the local funding environment, the local office decided that it would engage in local fund-raising. To achieve this, ITDG created what is perceived by Peruvian NGOs to be a virtual Peruvian organisation, with its own stationery and articles of association, and officially registered as a local NGO under Peruvian law. This virtual local organisation is, however, entirely controlled by its UK headquarters and is accountable not to a Peruvian Board, but to the UK Board of Trustees. So successful was this strategy that, in 1996, the local office was able to meet 60% of its operational and project costs, obtaining grants from a number of sources including FONCODES. There were plans in 1997 to raise more than 80% of its budget from local sources, and it has even been mooted that the local office will eventually be able to subsidise the operations of the UK headquarters, thus reversing the flow of aid funds from the South to the North.

Another example of a northern NGO making similar adjustments is Oxfam UKI. The organisation invested substantial resources in establishing a local presence for raising funds to compensate for declining income at home. This has enabled the local office to tap both multilateral sources and counterpart funds in Peru. Local NGOs have become increasingly concerned by these trends as they feel they are themselves unable to compete with institutions as well endowed and well equipped as Oxfam UKI. They criticise Oxfam UKI for back-tracking on its principles and values in order to access funds locally. They cite, for example, the fact that despite many years of criticising and campaigning against the policy of monetisation of food aid, Oxfam UKI has come to be silent on the matter so as to enable the local office to negotiate grants from monetised food aid in Peru. Such actions are viewed by many as opportunism by an organisation bent on ensuring its own institutional survival.

Other northern NGOs have chosen different strategies to compensate for declining incomes. Oxfam America, for example, has been working with local groups in the Amazon rain forests. To support this work it has sought to mobilise funds by negotiating debt swaps, and obtained funds from the Carbon Offset programme in which US coal-burning power stations are required to invest in protection of forests to offset increased carbon dioxide in the atmosphere. The US-based Catholic Relief Services (CRS) has been involved in Peru for many years, primarily as an agent for the US government agent for food aid. Since 1996, CRS has increasingly handed over responsibility for the administration of food aid to the local CARITAS. It has been transforming itself into a donor agency, with a growing interest in supporting work with credit. With the likelihood of continued congressional cuts to the US aid budget, it has been under pressure to raise funds from other sources, including accessing monetised food aid funds, counterpart funds and funds from multilateral agencies. CRS has also focused its attention on training local groups in participatory planning methods and in fund-raising, but also sees its role as helping local NGOs to negotiate substantial grants from international donor agencies.

PERSPECTIVES ON DIRECT FUNDING

The transformation of northern NGOs into intermediaries for official aid agencies or into competitors for funds in the local market is seen by many as evidence of 'the death of development as social transformation'. Their former commitment to the popular movement and to solidarity has been replaced by a culture of technical co-operation. The culture of partnership has been replaced by contract culture. As northern European NGOs have changed and absorbed the prevailing neo-liberal ideology of development as technical solutions we see 'the end of solidarity and the beginning of an era of pragmatism and efficiency'. Many Peruvian NGOs have been critical of what they perceive to be a failure on the part of northern NGOs to help build strong, viable and sustainable institutions, especially given the frequent claims made by northern NGOs about building institutional capacity.

The local director of one northern NGO expressed the view that the changes that have occurred in Peru have more to do with a crisis in ideology than as a result of changes in the funding environment. NGOs in Peru once had a clear vision about the social transformations they wanted to see. But with the collapse of popular movements and peasant unions, Peruvian NGOs have been deprived of their client base, their legitimacy and their *raison d'être*. NGOs had reacted to this, he thought, by becoming engaged in qualitatively different types of programme such as credit and welfare.

Many Peruvian NGOs were concerned that changes in funding patterns have nevertheless reified the depoliticisation of NGOs. NGOs were being encouraged to become instruments of economic and social stabilisation programmes. There was concern amongst some NGOs about the extent to which they had become service providers, carrying out work that some thought should be the responsibility of the state. The funds being made available by official agencies had been associated with an increasing trend towards NGOs being viewed as subcontractors to the aid agencies. NGOs were under pressure to become more professionalised and employ greater numbers of specialists. Grants made available by USAID, for example, to a feminist organisation (Manuela Ramos) involved in women's health had resulted in the organisation having to have a two-tier salary structure so as to employ professionals who were considered suitable by USAID. Those employed in the project had higher salaries than those employed by Manuela Ramos itself, which had resulted in a decline in staff morale.

Many Peruvian NGOs felt that the effect of their project activities on the quality of life of the poor had become less important to the official agencies than measures of project performance and keeping to schedules. 'They want irrigation canals to be completed on time, it is not important whether or not the peasants are going to use it', complained one informant. 'When you work for the [Counterpart] Fund you do not have time to think about what you are doing', said another. Efficient management of resources, measurable impacts (at least of the sort that satisfies the donor), cost-benefit analyses, logical frameworks: these are all part of the new language of development.

The sizeable grants that became available to the sector created anxieties about the extent to which local NGOs had become dependent on the aid agencies, and worries that such funds may disappear as quickly as they had appeared. Many NGOs had been created as a result of the kinds of funds that were available, and were operating largely as instruments of the aid agencies rather than responding to the needs and priorities of the poor. Many NGOs built their programmes around the idea of lobbying the state for resources with and on behalf of the poor. But as the state cut back on social expenditure, NGOs were increasingly being required to provide services in the place of the state.

Many NGOs were concerned that they had replaced the government as the principal partner of aid agencies. This has led to antagonism between NGOs and the government as a result of a perception that greater funds for NGOs meant fewer for government. NGOs were finding themselves competing with their government to get access to these new funds. Government officials felt that increased funding directly to the local NGOs has taken place at the expense of bilateral or inter-governmental co-operation. The government felt that the provision of funds by official donors directly to NGOs weakened the government's own influence and ability to control the direction of development. Suspicions prevailed about the intentions of donor agencies in using NGOs as a political tool, while the government was held in suspicion by the donor agencies for being corrupt, bureaucratic and unaccountable.

Aid agencies have justified their enthusiasm for supporting NGOs as a means for strengthening civil society. But civil society is not synonymous with NGOs, it includes other organisations in society such as trade unions, peasant organisations and political formations, as well as the business sector. Not all of these sectors have been the recipients of the generosity of the aid agencies. The selectivity of their generosity has resulted in distortions of the nature of civil society and a shaping of the structures of civil society that reflects more the prejudices of the official aid agencies than anything organic to the culture and history of Peru. The collapse of the popular movements in Peru, with whom many NGOs were linked, has led to a certain crisis and the creation of a political vacuum. The role which NGOs played in supporting civil society through these popular movements in the past has been replaced by new politically conservative organisations supported by the official aid agencies with their obsession with the growing role of private enterprise matched with the declining role of the state.

CONCLUSION

The NGO sector in Peru has long been characterised by the quality of its intellectual output and its innovative ideas which established it as a world leader in the 1970s. The sector suffered many severe shocks, through the economic collapse of the country and the civil war where it became not only incapable of stopping the violence but also its target. In the 1990s some of these pressures were reduced, but they then faced the new funding environment in which vast amounts of funds were made available to a sector that was ill prepared to cope, and which was only beginning to emerge from the period of repression. The net impact of these events has been to dilute the sector's earlier strong vision of development as a means for social transformation to one that is dominated by a funding-led development agenda. There has been huge growth in the number of NGOs, stimulated by the availability of money. NGOs increasingly have to become professionalised service deliverers, subcontracting to their clients, the donor agencies. The effect has not been confined to Peruvian NGOs who are beginning to face competition from northern NGOs for the same resources. Although the availability of substantial funds has had an important influence on the changing profile of the NGO sector, it does not necessarily account for all the changes seen during the 1990s. It is not entirely clear that the growth of NGOs has resulted in the strengthening of civil society: it might be argued that the shape of civil society has been distorted to accommodate the views of civil society of the more powerful of the official aid agencies.

Chapter 4

Kenya: A Political Agenda

ECONOMIC BACKGROUND

In many respects Kenya's political economy has been a major factor in its impaired ability to generate an acceptable standard of living for its people. While yielding Kenya's best ever economic performance in the decade following independence, the new economic growth model was unable to deliver on the promise of high and growing per capita incomes, equitably distributed so that all are free from want, disease and exploitation made at independence (Osodo and Matsvai 1998). Subsequent development plans entrenched a growing degree of inequality in Kenya, despite wide-ranging policies and measures to revamp the economy, generate employment and alleviate poverty. The economy remained unsteady, declining in the period after the late 1970s. This decline took place as the country's population growth rate remained among the highest in the world, reaching 4% around the mid-1980s.

Lack of productive employment opportunities on farms and elsewhere, in the face of rapid growth of the labour force, resulted in a fall in real wages in most sectors of the economy with urban unemployment rising from 11% in 1977 to 16% in 1986 and to 22% in 1992. Reflecting this rising unemployment was an increase in urban poverty estimated at nearly 30% in 1992. In rural areas, the average per capita holding in the smallholder sector declined from two hectares to 1.6 hectares during 1982–92, increasing the percentage of households with little or no land, and maintaining the incidence of rural poverty at 47% during the same period. Overall, some 10.3 million (43% of the population) people were classified as poor in Kenya in 1992.

Reflecting the overall decline in the economy was a growing decline in private investment and in public spending on social services. Investment as a proportion of gross domestic product (GDP) fell from 26% to 22% between 1978 and 1988. While reflecting the changing trends in the economy, overall public expenditure in both education and health remained low in real terms throughout the 1980s. To maintain these and other basic social services, the government was forced into further borrowing, in return pledging to continue its commitment to structural adjustment with the implementation of reforms. This resulted in further government withdrawal from basic service provision. Increasingly it became necessary for other actors to fill the gap left by a retreating state. For the first time, publicly and through its sessional and other planning documents, the government called on the private voluntary sector to come to its support, acknowledging its role in development and delineating specific socio-economic areas in which it was needed. This is the overall context that saw NGOs emerge as major players within Kenya's development and civic space.

NGOS IN KENYA

Organised welfarism and voluntarism in Kenya predated the colonial state and were core to traditional African associational life as well as to its socio-political and economic interaction. However, civic organisations in Kenya were strongly shaped by colonialism, the post-independence politics of development and the funding priorities and practices of northern development agencies. This influence has given rise to an NGO sector that contains both local and foreign elements.

In this study, the term NGO is used to embrace a broad range of voluntary, non-profit development organisations operating outside the state, but in the public sphere. A distinction is made between the formally constituted non-profit organisations which provide development services to, or work on the behalf of, the needy and the formal and informal organisations created by needy people themselves for their own benefit. NGOs in Kenya may be broadly classified as:

Service or *Intermediary* NGOs, set up for and usually not controlled by the targeted beneficiaries. Commonly these are legally registered organisations with paid staff, providing development services in areas such as improved natural resource management, health care, information, education and credit. Included here are Kenyan indigenous organisations such as Undugu Society of Kenya and Kenya Rural Enterprise Programme (K-REP) as well as indigenous and local branches of European NGOs such as Action Aid–Kenya.

Horizontal NGOs, not reaching into the community level. These organisations exist as co-ordinators of, or providers to, other organisations. Examples of such organisations include the National Council of NGOs and the National Council of Women of Kenya. Other horizontal organisations are sectorally oriented, such as the Population Council and the Family Planning Association Kenya (FPAK). Functionally, horizontal organisations assist intermediaries or the NGO sphere overall in the following ways: providing funding or other technical support services, facilitating exchange of experience and brokering alliances. They also advocate sectoral interests in NGOs overall or for changes in policies, laws and institutions that constrain development, or that are inimical to social justice and human rights.

Community Membership-based People's Organisations, created and controlled by individuals to advance their own interests. Included here is the formal (in the sense of being registered and recognised by the state's development system) and the traditional informal mutual assistance and self-help groups such as women's groups, youth clubs and the 'merry-go-rounds and mutual saving schemes'. These straddle urban and rural areas of Kenya and are currently estimated to number between 30,000 and 40,000. Many of these groups grow into bigger organisations, acquiring staff and providing services to members and others. Examples of such membership service organisations include a host of co-operatives and other professional associations found in Kenya today.

Religious/Church-based Organisations, operating as development departments and institutions (under the various religious groups or as ecumenical bodies) and providing similar development services. The development departments of the Catholic dioceses in Kenya and the national Council of Churches of Kenya fall within this category.

In Kenya, formal non-state Western-styled welfare delivery systems were established early in the century with the advent of missionaries who accompanied the colonialists. The earliest of these included the Presbyterian Church of East Africa who came at the invitation of the British East Africa Company in 1891, the Salvation Army in 1921 and the YMCA and YWCA, founded in 1910 and 1920 respectively. The post-Second World War period saw the emergence of a new class of organisations with a service orientation shifting their attention from charitable activities in the North to similar activities in the South, now referred to as relief and development. Examples include organisations such as OXFAM and CARE.

Such organisations brought a new NGO model with them, on the one hand supportive of the colonial powers, while on the other autonomous in perspectives and actions. Towards independence, a number of local NGOs were established on this model. The African Medical and Research Foundation (AMREF) founded in 1957, which focused on providing health care, was one such organisation. A number of church and church-based institutions also adopted this model, expanding their activities to include relief and other aspects of development. The Christian Council of Kenya (CCK), later renamed NCCK, not only provided relief and development services, but also lobbied the colonial state on justice and human rights issues.

At independence, some forty-five NGOs were operational in Kenya, of which nearly a third were foreign, northern-based NGOs. Independence ushered in a new era for NGOs in Kenya. The immediate post-independence development paradigm associated the problem of development with lack of resources and knowledge. NGOs adopted a basic needs approach in addressing what they perceived to be the pressing problems of development. NGOs were largely viewed by the new regime as apolitical and as sources of necessary additional capital to support pursuits of patronage. This benign attitude towards NGOs encouraged a fourfold growth of the sector in the decade following independence, with foreign NGOs comprising almost half the total number of organisations.

Between 1978 and 1988 the number of NGOs in Kenya increased by 102% from 132 to 267, with foreign NGOs growing at nearly double the rate of local NGOs. However, this trend changed during the period 1988–96 which saw local NGOs growing by 131%, nearly tripling the rate of growth in the number of foreign NGOs. This data is based on information regarding officially registered or recognised NGOs: unofficially it is estimated that there were between 3,000 and 3,500 NGOs operating in Kenya by 1997.

This growth was engendered by the channelling of substantial funds towards the sector and by donor agencies' attempts to reduce the role of the state in service provision. Growing awareness of issues such as the environment, human rights, democratisation and gender (particularly following the 1985 women's decade meeting in Nairobi) also contributed to the proliferation of NGOs during this period.

The role of NGOs in the fields of education, health, welfare and relief, water and micro-enterprise development in Kenya has been substantial. In 1989 it was estimated that NGOs in the health sector provided up to 40% of health facilities and between 40–50% of all family planning services in the country. Almost 45% of all village polytechnics in the country were initiated and supported by NGOs (Ng'ethe and Kanyinga 1992). Some US$125–230 million come to Kenya through NGOs annually, representing an estimated 12–25% of total external resource allocation to Kenya (FEMNET 1989; Ng'ethe and Kanyinga 1992; Fowler 1993; *Daily Nation*, 2 November 1996). This total includes an estimated US$150 million coming through religious organisations (Waithaka and Glaesor 1991). More than 30,000 membership groups and associations throughout the country have been involved in the provision of services, mobilising resources, originating, implementing and managing wide-ranging development initiatives.

NGOS AND THE STATE

The colonial period saw the emergence of many ethnic and trans-ethnic associations, confronting and lobbying the colonial state on a wide range of social, political and economic injustices to which Africans were subjected. It also saw consistent attempts by the colonial state to undermine and constrict this indigenous civil associational life, as part of a broad strategy to consolidate colonial domination. Many of these associations were frequently proscribed or relegated to play marginal roles. However, they continued to organise, sometimes along ethnic lines, intensifying the move towards independence and preparing the ground for many of the pre- and post-independence activist and nationalist movements (Nyangira 1987). The labour movement, which eventually became closely allied to the nationalist movement, was particularly notable for its role in challenging injustice and campaigning for social and economic reforms. Churches and church-based organisations at that time generally played a reactionary role, aligning themselves with the colonial power and condemning any independent activism.

The post-independence era saw two parallel developments in the relationship between the state and organisations of civil society. The state recognised the social and economic benefits which accrued as a result of the work of NGOs. At the same time it grew wary of their growth and sought to control and limit their role within predefined notions of nation-building. Thus while welfare and development NGOs were promoted and grew in numbers during the Kenyatta regime, civil organisations formally opposed to the regime's excesses and seeking social, economic and political reforms were enfeebled either through co-option, reshaping or outright proscription. For example, the trade union movement was once the most powerful expression of civic organisation with any ability to keep state power under check. Its growing popular and political base at a time when the Kenyatta regime was increasingly centralising its power, was seen as a threat. The regime passed legislation to collapse the entire trade union movement into one body, the Central Organisation of Trade Unions (COTU) which was officially affiliated to the ruling party Kenya Africa National Union (KANU).

The muzzling of civil associational life was exacerbated following the proscription, in 1969, of the Kenya People's Union (KPU), making Kenya a *de facto* one-party state. The 1970s witnessed minimal challenges to state excesses, except from staff and student unions at the University of Nairobi. The period saw the emergence of clandestine organisations such as Mwakenya, the December 12 Movement, the Kenya Anti-Imperialist Front and the London-based Committee for the Release of Political Prisoners in Kenya (Ongwen 1996).

Following the death of Kenyatta, Moi was established as the president of a country that was already ethnically divided. Moi's first broad strategy entailed the dismantling of affective networks which had been formed to advance Kikuyu political and economic interests. The second strategy, effected simultaneously, entailed the construction of a new loyal coalition, drawn first and largely from members of his own ethnic Kalenjin community. Following a failed coup attempt in 1982 lead by disaffected junior officers in the air force, all forms of opposition were brutally suppressed, and Moi set about reinventing KANU, through constitutional amendment, as an institution for political brokerage and a vehicle for suppressing opponents or critics of the government. By 1985, growing incidences of political suppression and human rights violations, corruption and other forms of social abuses, prompted other civil society actors (notably the church, church-based institutions and professional bodies) to focus on issues of social, economic and political justice and to demand reforms of the state. The Kenya Episcopal Conference, NCCK and some of its affiliated churches such as the Church of the Province of Kenya (CPK) and the Law Society of Kenya became notable activists for change during this period.

Meanwhile many in the international community were beginning to express concerns about repression and the performance of the state, and were calling for the establishment of a more plural society to stave off the mounting threat of dissent against the regime. As part of that strategy, relatively substantial resources were increasingly made available to NGOs while funding through the state diminished. This resulted in further growth of the NGO sector, with many NGOs extending their scope to incorporate a democracy and governance agenda. Pressure on the state for social, economic and political reforms intensified.

The state, for its part, became increasingly worried about its lack of access to and control over resources and the power and autonomy which access to resources endowed on civil institutions. In 1986, in its first attempt to co-ordinate the work of NGOs, the state issued an edict that NGOs at the local level would have to liaise and clear their projects and budgets with the government-controlled local District Development Committees (DDC). NGOs at the national level were required to do the same with the treasury and planning ministry. In the same year, Kenya's largest women's organisation, Maendeleo ya Wanawake, was officially affiliated to the ruling party KANU, as a means of controlling its activities. At the same time, on the pretext that some NGOs were subversive, a presidential decree was issued requiring all future NGO funding to be channelled through the government (Ndegwa 1993). An unsuccessful bid was made the following year requiring NGOs to register with the treasury.

Meanwhile individual NGOs continued to oppose such attempts to control them. Fiery confrontation between the government and two NGOs galvanised government resolve to strengthen its control over NGOs: there was tension with the NCCK in 1986 over opposition to the introduction of queue-voting in the elections, and with the environmental NGO Greenbelt Movement in 1989 over a government plan to build on public recreation ground. A presidential decree issued in 1989, aimed at co-ordinating and controlling NGOs, sought to ensure that their activities were consistent with what the regime defined as 'in the national interest'. This culminated in the NGO Co-ordination Bill, hurriedly conceived and tabled in Parliament in 1990 and passed into law the following year. The bill allowed for, amongst other things, the de-registration of errant NGOs, the establishment of a government NGO Bureau to oversee NGO administration (including registration and co-ordination) and the creation of a national council of NGOs to serve as a self-regulatory body for the sector (Ng'ethe and Kanyinga 1992; Ndegwa 1993).

Within the NGO community the bill was seen as fundamentally flawed and a tool to restrict and control rather than regulate NGOs. The bill drew sharp criticism from a broad section of NGOs and, for the first time, pulled the sector together in a collective engagement with the state. A seminar was organised by the Institute of Development Studies of the University of Nairobi and the moribund NGO umbrella body, the Kenya National Council of Social Services, where some 130 NGOs constituted themselves into a loose network and formed a ten-member NGO Standing Committee (NGOSC). The Standing Committee was mandated to present to government a common sector position on the Act and to engage in a dialogue with government regarding the provisions of the Act, thus ensuring that NGOs' interests were taken into account (NGOSC Concerns 1991; Ndegwa 1993). Eight national consultative conventions were held between 1991 and 1993, and lengthy meetings with the government ultimately yielded appropriate concessions and amendments to the Act. In March 1993, the NGO Act finally came into force. An NGO Co-ordination Bureau was launched as the legitimate body for registering NGOs under the Act. The same year also saw the birth of the National Council of NGOs as the legitimate representative of NGOs and the principal basis for negotiations between the sector, the state and international bodies.

It is notable that several international agencies, in particular USAID, UNEP, UNDP, the Ford Foundation and the World Bank, played important roles in this process by supporting the NGO network and providing material resources. Such moves had come in the wake of the decision by a number of multilateral and bilateral agencies, one year previously, to withdraw aid from Kenya, a decision that forced the regime to permit the activities of other political parties. The NGO Co-ordination Act marked a major turning point in the relationships both amongst NGOs and between the NGO sector and the state, for the first time providing an institutional framework within which the membership could not only register under a common legal regime, but also engage with other stakeholders and advance shared goals.

The NGO Co-ordination Act has not, however, provided complete protection and autonomy to the sector. Certain instruments of control and intimidation still contained in the Act place NGOs in a particularly vulnerable position *vis-à-vis* the state. The Registration Board has broad discretionary powers to accept or refuse applications for registration, and to withdraw previously granted certifications of NGOs whose activities are deemed inconsistent with national interest (section 14 of the Act). In February 1995, the legal and human rights NGO, the Centre for Law and Research International (CLARION), was deregistered on the grounds that it failed to adhere to the conditions under which it had registered barely a year previously. Mwangaza Trust, another civic body was similarly deregistered only a month before CLARION's deregistration. These two cases serve to indicate that the space in which civil society organisations operate remains restricted, particularly for those which represent views regarded as dissenting or otherwise inimical to the interests of the government.

DONOR AGENCY FUNDING TO THE NGO SECTOR

Official aid to Kenya, civil society organisations and NGOs in particular, has been inspired by the same neo-liberal development orthodoxy that has pervaded development thinking and practice since the beginning of the 1980s. According to this orthodoxy pluralist politics is necessary for a thriving free-market economy, and political and economic freedom of the individual constitutes the essential prerequisite for development. Civil society institutions, and in particular NGOs, are viewed as being at the forefront of efforts to establish democracy, and are the favoured partners for development.

Donor agencies claimed to experience growing disillusionment with the capacity of the state to facilitate development. They sought to achieve, through the use of instruments such as the economic structural adjustment programmes, a reduction of the role of the state in the economy and in service provision. The private sector and NGOs have been seen by these agencies as the purveyors of economic growth. Consequently, official agency support and funding have gradually been re-routed to NGOs, leading to a massive proliferation of NGOs, especially in the service sectors, an area from which the state has been encouraged to retreat. NGOs have been viewed by donor agencies as instruments for the provision of services that would, in particular, mitigate the impact of structural adjustment programmes on vulnerable groups.

Broadly, direct official funding to Kenyan NGOs has been either thematic or sectoral, reflecting the priorities and interests of the particular donor. Since the early 1990s, these interests and priorities have focused on enhancing good governance, democratisation and human rights, securing swift economic growth stewarded by the private sector, and containing Kenya's rapid population growth. Direct official funding to Kenyan NGOs has, in some cases, outstripped total disbursements to the government. The level of direct funding for democracy, governance and human rights has shown the largest increase from official sources.

USAID: USAID official funding to Kenya focuses primarily on controlling national population growth and the promotion of public health, increasing the commercialisation of small-scale agriculture, and creating an effective demand for sustainable political, constitutional and legal reform (USAID 1996). All USAID funding to Kenyan NGOs is delivered through the local USAID office either directly or via the government of Kenya and US Private Voluntary Organisations (PVOs).

Overall, total USAID budgetary allocations have remained relatively steady between 1991 and 1995, but in 1996 funds to Kenya decreased by 48%. Cumulative disbursements of programme funds on the other hand have progressively declined since 1992. This decline followed the general freezing of aid to Kenya by the bilateral donors in 1992. A rise in 1995 was the result of disbursement to the government of some US$2 million in non-project assistance for the Kenya Healthcare Finance programme. The funds were a carry-over from the same programme in fiscal year 1989 and therefore represented no real increase in funding to the government. However, direct funding to Kenyan NGOs doubled between 1992 and 1994. Jointly with American private institutions and universities, funding for NGOs and PVOs accounted for some 61% of total USAID cumulative programme disbursement in Kenya in 1995. The health and population sector since 1991 remains the lead recipient of USAID direct funding, followed by private enterprise, democracy and governance.

Democracy and governance have been themes of growing importance since 1994. Total programme funding over the period 1994–6 rose from a mere US$400,000 (1% of overall operational year budget) in 1994, to US$2 million (11%) in 1996. The programme has been singled out as the lead determinant in the US relationship and the USAID bilateral funding to Kenya in the period leading to and after the 1997 general elections (USAID 1996). In the event that the government of Kenya undertook more than incremental progress towards reforms for the 1997 general elections, the mission proposed restoration of some of the programme cuts in recent years to a level of at least US$25 million per year. Funding within this theme has been and will continue to be administered largely through local civil society NGOs.

DFID: DFID funding to Kenyan NGOs complements the British Government's priority in Kenya, namely the advancement of economic reforms. It also channels resources to NGO service delivery projects in health, education and governance. Kenyan NGOs are funded directly under respective programmes within DFID, via the government or local intermediaries of British NGOs. The British Government is the third highest bilateral donor to Kenya. However, unlike other donors, its share of total official development assistance to Kenya has shown only a slight decline during the 1990s.[1]

The bulk of British aid to Kenya has been channelled to the government in support of public sector reforms, the rehabilitation of infrastructure and the improvement of health, population and education services. Direct funding to Kenyan NGOs is a relatively recent phenomenon for DFID, commencing in late 1993. Direct funding to NGOs as a proportion of total DFID bilateral aid to Kenya was approximately 26% in 1994/5 (US$92,340,000).

CIDA: CIDA has supported structural and economic adjustment programmes, and activities associated with food security, environmental sustainability, human rights including increased participation of women in development, democratisation and good governance. Until its dissolution in April 1995, Partnership Africa Canada (PAC) was CIDA's vehicle for funding Kenyan NGOs. Since then CIDA funds to Kenyan NGOs have been channelled directly through the Canadian Embassy. The Canada Fund in Kenya has provided £50,000–£100,000 per annum non-thematic funds for local NGO initiatives in the 1990s. This does not cover NGO running costs and is granted on a one-off basis, although NGOs may reapply after some years. In 1997 CIDA introduced a new embassy fund named Agenda Equity, with an allocation of CAD$5 million for more than five years available to NGOs promoting women's initiatives. CIDA's total disbursement to Kenyan NGOs since 1993 has been maintained at around CAD$700,000.

SIDA: SIDA assistance has focused on rural health, rural water and sanitation, soil conservation and minor roads. A small but growing proportion of Swedish funding has been directed towards human rights, democratisation activities and good governance. SIDA funding has declined since 1990 from SEK150 million to SEK65 million, but is expected to remain at that level for the foreseeable future. SIDA has, however, allocated additional funds for research, the environment, disaster relief, human rights and advocacy, as well as providing official development assistance via Swedish NGOs. Total disbursements under this programme in 1994–5 was SEK61.1 million, of which the Swedish NGOs took

[1] In 1992/3 DFID funding to Kenya was UK£35,712 thousand but by 1996/7 had fallen to UK£26,096 thousand (DFID 1997).

some 42%. Although SIDA has shown a growing inclination to work with and directly fund local NGOs, this support has remained small and the government continues to be the major recipient of SIDA funds in Kenya. For instance under the 1995–8 development co-operation agreement with the government, only SEK29.35 million (1.3%) of the SEK2,275 million planned allocation to Kenya is targeted for direct disbursement to NGOs. Although this percentage is low relative to the total country frame budget, it represented a significant rise in total allocation to NGOs and will, over the three-year planned period, exceed total operational allocation to the government by about 3.2%.

The recipients will be NGOs in the water sector where SIDA has enjoyed a long-standing relationship of working with and funding local NGOs directly. The increase in allocation to NGOs follows recent restructuring within SIDA's water sector, which has added a new pilot programme to the water component. The restructuring was prompted partly by SIDA's lack of adequate capacity to administer the NGO projects, and partly by the need to ensure consistency with a recently restructured Ministry of Water Development, which now seeks to transfer the responsibility for implementing and managing water resources to the communities through self-help groups. SIDA has traditionally funded two community components under its water sector, one managed by the government and the other by NGOs, both on a 3:1 co-financing agreement, including local community contributions.

The new programme will operate under the district focus framework, with the district-level administrative staff advising the community groups on management issues and on selection and presentation of suitable projects for funding. The importance attached to human rights and democratisation by SIDA is reflected in the increased allocation of SEK2.2 million to SEK5 million during the 1993/4 and 1995/6 financial years respectively. All the funding has been given to Kenyan NGOs.

DANIDA: DANIDA funding to Kenyan NGOs has traditionally focused on small-scale agriculture, environment and health sectors. Like most other official donors, they have also increasingly emphasised human rights and good governance. Danish official funding to Kenya declined from DKr265 million in 1990 to DKr128.4 million in 1995. DANIDA's local grant authority to Kenyan NGOs has been approximately 10% of total Danish development assistance to Kenya. In 1997 this amounted to about DKr13 million. DANIDA has, however, been unable to use all the money set aside for NGOs owing to insufficient capacity to cope adequately with the resource demand in NGO work. DANIDA has chosen to work closely with Kenyan NGOs, particularly those involved in democracy and human rights programmes.

PERSPECTIVES ON DIRECT FUNDING

The decision in 1991 to freeze aid to Kenya was demonstrative of donors' lack of faith in the ability of the government to deliver services to the Kenyan people. In 1995 donor dissatisfaction meant that only 25% of total project aid to Kenya passed through the government, with the bulk of support going directly to donor-identified projects outside the government system. For bilateral donors the figure was 10% (Githu 1995).

Most official agencies cited the following reasons for their disinclination to provide funding to the government: continued muzzling of the press; limitations of political rights, human rights abuses; harassment of opposition politicians; repression of civic rights and limits on freedom of association; lack of an independent judiciary; lack of freedom of discussion in the national assembly; lack of government transparency and accountability; failure to make investments according to developmental priorities; decision-making without reference to parliament; lack of public access to information; corruption within public institutions; excessive bureaucratic procedures; unacceptable delays in implementation of donor-funded projects; poor capacity; lack of professionalism; poor project conception and execution; and high failure rates of donor projects.

Faced with these problems in their relationship with the government, most donors chose to channel their funds to NGOs. SIDA, for example, cited the government's poor capacity for effective implementation at the micro-level as its reason for choosing NGOs to implement water sector operations. Other donors, particularly those funding projects in health and population and the micro-enterprise sector, have insisted as part of their bilateral agreement with government that creditable NGOs within these sectors be subcontracted to implement projects for which they have funded the government. NGOs within these sectors have, the donors feel, demonstrated clear comparative advantage *vis-à-vis* the government in the delivery of family planning and child survival services to the most needy segments of the Kenyan population, and in empowering women by increasingly granting them the opportunity to participate in the development process. However, the biggest contribution NGOs have made has been in the areas of democracy, governance and human rights. The sector is vibrant, and contributes substantially to the nature of the debate on democratisation and governance in Kenya.

NGOs have been under pressure to demonstrate credibility in those areas in which government efforts have been criticised. A recently completed USAID assessment of democracy and governance in Kenya pointed out fundamental weaknesses among NGOs in the field of democracy and human rights. A large number of them are alleged to lack both roots in rural areas and established relationships with public sector actors. In the human rights and legal sector, NGOs

67

have been concentrated in Nairobi and have tended to be dominated, it was claimed, by a particular ethnic group. This ethnic bias has led to, according to the report, a loss of credibility and legitimacy from the general public and the government. The assessment also revealed that most NGOs have limited capacity, experience problems of transparency and accountability and suffer from organisational and managerial weaknesses (USAID 1996). This view is confirmed by other studies commissioned by donors (e.g. Ikiara and Tostensen 1995; Krystal, Waithaka and Young 1995). There is a growing feeling amongst some donors that NGOs are becoming an alternative form of private accumulation for those who do not have access to the market or the state.

While the government has in recent years sought to promote expanded NGO involvement in the development process, most donors consider that they do so with reluctance and only because of mounting pressures. The government is perceived as always having been hostile to direct funding generally but specifically to the funding of those NGOs engaged in the field of democracy and governance and human rights, which it has often branded as 'subversive' and 'servants of foreign masters'. In one extreme case, NORAD's decision to focus on human rights resulted in a diplomatic crisis and subsequent expulsion of the agency from Kenya in 1990. The Norwegian government has not given a cent to the Kenya government since.

Kenyan NGOs are considered by official agencies to be better placed than either the government or northern NGOs to develop into effective development actors. Their smallness, flexibility, ability to innovate and responsiveness is thought to give them a comparative advantage in micro-development over government, northern NGOs and the donors themselves. Their small size is considered favourable to ensuring lower overheads and a more administratively manageable organisation. The active involvement of Kenyan NGOs has been identified as critical to the overall success of a poverty alleviation strategy, as well as in facilitating the successful identification, execution and monitoring of poverty-focused interventions. On the issues of democracy, governance and human rights, although vulnerable, local NGOs are considered well placed in the long term to press for and influence a broad-based agenda for sustainable reforms, because of their natural location within Kenya's civil society. However, corruption, which had resulted in the loss of faith in the government, is viewed as an increasingly common phenomenon amongst local NGOs, and was often cited as the cause for damaging the value of local NGOs *vis-à-vis* northern NGOs. Opportunistic or 'brief-case' NGOs, formed by individuals who see establishing an NGO as an expedient means of raising money, have become a common feature of the sector in recent years, resulting in a further erosion of donor trust in local NGOs.

The government's view is that while direct funding to NGOs has some benefits, it has also created problems. Government has little sense of 'ownership' of projects, some of which it must assume responsibility for. Government officers have been used to viewing all expenditure outside government control as illegal, and believed under donor project conditions this has tended to predispose NGOs to corruption. The government has felt that there are certain functions that NGOs cannot perform, as many of them have limited capacities. Many of the financial accounting and control problems that beset government have, they believe, reappeared in NGOs. A practical problem for the government has been in the variety of aid agencies with which it has had to deal, each having its own set of regulations, procedures for reporting and accounting and different conditions for granting aid. The diverse systems for disbursing funds, the different forms required and the range of accounting systems have been bewildering to officers attempting to implement projects. Furthermore, individual donors have their own priority for funding (or not funding) activities and have set their own criteria for designing and appraising projects, criteria with which the government implementing agency has not always agreed. Preparatory work on donor-funded projects has often been carried out without reference to government and institutions. The incidence of inappropriate designs and 'white elephants' has been, government officials feel, more common. Sometimes the need to expend aid agency budgets has overruled careful identification and preparation. However, the government has also admitted that sometimes it appeared too ready to sign agreements without adequately considering the long-term implications or likely demands after implementation.

Official agency direct funding to NGOs has been directed primarily towards the larger NGOs. They are considered to have proven track records in relation to competence in aid delivery and the requisite managerial and financial skills. Few local NGOs meet these criteria and the biggest task for official agencies has been screening to find reliable or fundable local NGOs. Aid agencies often expressed shock at the level of administrative incompetence and corruption amongst some local NGOs. One agency official from SIDA indicated that 75% of her time was spent administering Swedish SEK3 million among 10–15 local NGOs while the much larger health projects (to a total of SEK38 million) took up only about 20% of her time. Similar administrative pressures in dealing with local NGOs are described by USAID officials, particularly those dealing with NGOs in the field of democracy and human rights. Often, many of the actors are either new or unknown, accounting systems are not in place, the amounts involved are small and evaluation systems practically non-existent.

One consequence of weak capacity amongst most local NGOs is that the majority of aid agencies have been unable to spend the budget earmarked for local NGOs. As a result, there has been a tendency to over-fund a small and select group of creditable NGOs. Many of these NGOs pointed to incidences where they had been wooed by donors into accepting more funds. A disproportionate amount of official aid has therefore gone to their local affiliates, northern NGOs.

A number of foreign NGOs have taken the opportunities that the new funding environment has provided for them. There has therefore been a tendency for northern NGOs to establish a locally registered NGO out of expediency. With a substantial infrastructure and resource base at home and long-standing experience of working in those areas in which donors have an interest, they have been able to attract funding from donor agencies who have been anxious to disburse their budget allocation to local NGOs. Some NGOs (such as AMREF) have presented themselves as local NGOs, although in reality they are international organisations with offices in several different countries, including the UK. Dual status as local and international NGO has enabled these NGOs to tap resources in either guise.

There has been much criticism of what has been described as the paternalistic and patronising 'big brother' attitude amongst northern NGOs when dealing with local counterparts. This attitude has, many feel, created dependency and amounts to failure to have built local capacities for self-learning, enterprise and growth. One USAID officer related two scenarios of his experience of direct funding. In one scenario he secured a partnership in which the beneficiary was a small local NGO, however a US PVO received the money, approved expenditure and accounted directly to USAID for the project activities. In another partnership the local NGO received funds directly, made decisions and accounted directly to USAID on the application of funds and the daily management of the project. The US PVO's role was one of providing stewardship and helping develop key competencies needed for the effective running of the project. In the former case the local NGO emerged as underdog, often very passive at meetings and tending to go along with what big brother said. There was no partnership. In the latter case the local NGO was accountable for its decisions as the implementing agency and felt in charge. An incremental improvement in its capacity to run, discuss, innovate and make necessary adjustments in the course of implementation was indicative of a maturing partnership relationship, not only with USAID but also with the US PVO. This relationship went beyond the mere routing or transfer of funds. It was consistent with the views expressed by a number of official donors that northern NGOs were perhaps better placed to help in the strengthening of organisational and institutional capacities of local NGOs, but rarely played such a role.

THE IMPACT OF DIRECT FUNDING

Institutionally, Kenyan NGOs have a limited absorptive capacity, weak delivery mechanisms, inadequate technical expertise and managerial effectiveness, and are unable to report satisfactorily on their performance use of project funds. Consequently they have not met official donor demands for their services. The ability of local NGOs to mobilise resources for their work is generally less developed compared with that of their northern counterparts. The resulting over-dependence on foreign donors has weakened their bargaining base, reducing their capacity to influence the agenda and increasing their vulnerability to manipulation by some donors.

There is concern among Kenyan NGOs about the increasingly contractual nature of direct funding. Official aid in the 1990s has become an instrument to ensure that the development process and its outcomes are consistent with the expectation of the new global order. This is reflected in the increasing casual application of externally demanded conditionalities. Those who receive grants from official aid are increasingly faced with complex reporting procedures and have to comply with regulations to an extent that they feel detracts from their work.

Although the volume of funding available to the NGO sector has grown, the larger grants have most often been provided to northern NGOs, or international NGOs (such as AMREF which has a UK base), either directly, or through satellite institutions. The only exception to this is in the case of large grants for human rights and democracy, for which local NGOs are usually the main recipients. The main reason for this has been the apparently weak infrastructure of many local NGOs. Although many donors have recognised the importance of capacity-building, the investment made in so doing has been limited.

Many local NGOs complain about the failure of northern NGOs to help Kenyans build effective organisations. This is despite northern NGOs raising much of their money on the basis of their claims for doing so. Kenyan NGOs feel that northern NGOs have not delivered on partnership. Northern NGOs, one respondent commented, need to work on influencing policy in their own backyard. Currently northern NGOs use southern NGOs as a justification for funding. Some northern NGOs, such as ActionAid, have received grants from DFID to provide institutional strengthening of local NGOs.

Many express concern that northern NGOs behave in a manner which is just as heavy-handed, strict and inflexible as that of official donor agencies. Nevertheless, many also believe that co-operation with northern NGOs had in the past enabled work to be undertaken that is increasingly difficult to carry out with the support of official agencies.

Box 4.1: Kenya Energy and Environmental Organisation (KENGO)

KENGO developed an ecological and cultural model for sustainable liveli-
hoods after consultation with its grass-roots-based members' organisations
in 1993. In this model (the Uhai model) grass-roots communities were to
be organised in regional and community forums, as a means of holding
KENGO more accountable to their needs. The Uhai model was considered
radical and was an approach which KENGO's northern partners did not
particularly like. Up until 1992, KENGO enjoyed significant amounts of
funding from both northern NGOs and directly from official agencies.
KENGO's proposal to its official agency partners in 1993 was received
unfavourably, viewed by the official agencies almost as a negation of the
purpose of funding over the previous seven years. The proposal was
rejected by the four official agency partners. KENGO was left then with a
cynical perception of official agencies: KENGO's experience is that the
official agencies will not give direct funding to southern NGOs and CBOs
if this ultimately results in independence. The former relationship with the
official agencies had been a contractual one and proposals were submitted
within the official agencies' agendas. One representative of an NGO summarised his experience as follows: 'we cannot blame them [official agen-
cies], because we never said "no". We had direct funding, until you questioned there was no problem. Direct funding is the most pervasive form of
funding, but bilateral funding has a powerful political agenda. Every
Western government has an agenda to sell. The southern NGO becomes a
conduit for that agenda. The challenge to southern intermediaries, the
government or NGOs, is to get the resources and create a local agenda.
Money from official agencies comes within a framework that is short-term
oriented, but you cannot begin to nurture a local agenda.'

The impact of selective direct funding has been a reduction in the level of
funding available to the smaller NGOs who operate in areas not considered to
be a priority area of interest to the donors. Many of them have had to either
reduce the scale of their activities or incorporate new agendas more pleasing to
the official donors with the risk of being diverted away from their own missions
and losing their institutional identities. In many cases, they have simply had to
close down. This has clearly been the case with many NGOs involved in general integrated development and in particular those in agriculture, environment,
community social awareness and education activities, and those located in rural
areas. Many of these NGOs have traditionally received the bulk of their fund-

ing from northern NGO partners. Growing pressure on the latter to show 'successful' projects in the South, coupled with weakening public social morality and obligation towards private giving in the North, has resulted in many of these NGOs being marginalised (Fowler 1994, 1995; Wolfe 1989). The overall impact on the sector has been a tendency towards organisational convergence and a narrowing of the scope of local NGO activity. This has resulted in reduced diversity and innovation, and the emergence of an NGO sector that is donor-moulded and resource-led rather than socially responsive. It has become increasingly dominated by large, service-delivery intermediary NGOs serving as subcontractors to official development agency policies. Inevitably there has been a shift in the locus of accountability for such NGOs – away from their constituencies and towards official donors – resulting in damage to the participatory and emancipatory ideals upon which reputations had, in many cases, originally been built.

Where direct funding had entered a particular sector, negative competition between NGOs was created through a proliferation of organisations in that sector and the undermining of existing, already stretched, governmental infrastructures. For example, a national consortium for NGOs, the National Council for Population Development (NCPD), working in the family planning and population sector, in the late 1980s, was housed under the Ministry of Health. As funding to the NGOs in this sector increased NCPD was overwhelmed, with the result that its activities were monopolised. The NGO functioned more as a conduit for bilateral funds to NGOs at a cost to its other co-ordinating and support role. NCPD became extremely bureaucratic and the result was that many NGOs disowned it, seeking alternative channels.

Some NGOs feel that direct funding has an adverse effect on the relationship between Kenyan NGOs and the government of Kenya. They believe that there are some basic services that the government should provide and the role of NGOs should be to supplement, not replace, these. The government is seen to be reaching a point where it is obliged to accept direct funding to Kenyan NGOs from official agencies. The way ahead, it is felt, should be a collaboration between southern NGOs and southern governments rather than a competition for funding from official agencies.

Kenyan NGOs feel that large amounts of funds released quickly in sums greater than the absorptive capacity of NGOs, has had the effect of inhibiting the natural and progressive growth of an NGO. For example, NCCK received such funding between 1992 and 1994 during a period of multiparty euphoria for democratisation (including election monitoring, civic and voter education) and ethnic clashes. NCCK expanded rapidly in terms of geographic spread, programmes and recruitment. This created problems for the organisation whose capacity to manage such large programmes had not yet been developed.

CONCLUSION

Official aid to Kenya has shrunk during the 1990s.[2] With the exception of British aid, there has been a general reduction in official aid directed to the government. Concurrently, there has been increased direct funding to local NGOs. This general trend appears set to continue, with indications pointing towards a stable or declining total official (bilateral) development assistance to Kenya, continued reductions to the government and a general increase in the level of overall direct funding to NGOs (both local and international).

This is clearly the case with SIDA and USAID support. A development corporation agreement between Kenya and Sweden covering the country programme for the period July 1995 to December 1998 stated that the country frame budget for Kenya will be US$36.5 million for the agreement period or US$10.4 million per twelve-month period. US$10.4 million for the 1995–6 budget year represents a decline of 19% from US$12.848 million the previous financial year (July 1995).

The total operational year budget allocations for USAID for 1996 of US$18.0 million represented a decline of about 50% from the 1995 allocation of US$34.4 million. This was expected either to stabilise at US$18 million annually until the year 2000 or to decline further depending on Kenya's performance in the three critical areas of US interest and priority in Kenya (USAID 1996). The ongoing restructuring and retrenchment at the CIDA Nairobi office are indicators that no changes are expected in the already minimal direct funding to Kenya by CIDA. Similar overall cuts were reportedly expected from DANIDA.

While improvements in Kenya's political and economic performance during 1997 have rekindled donor interest, particularly the multilateral donors including IMF and World Bank, who granted Kenya a 'clean bill of health' and restored funding to previous high levels, most bilateral donors have taken a 'wait-and-see' stance, with their eyes focused on events leading to and following the 1997 national general elections. The major immediate concern for most of them lies in ensuring free and fair elections and extending involvement of civil society actors in the political process. A major thrust of their bilateral support to the government subsequently consists of securing legal and constitutional reforms and good governance through funding and technical support to the judiciary (Attorney General's Chambers) and the parliament, the electoral commission and the office of the Controller and Auditor General (ODA 1995; SIDA 1996a; USAID 1996). Continued improvements within the health and population sector, where the government traditionally has been the major recipient of bilateral funding, remains an important strategic objective and an area for continued official support, as is ensuring continuity in the present path of economic reconstruction. However, these trends are expected to occur within the broad framework of a generally declining total official development assistance to Kenya.

Direct official support to NGOs on the other hand appeared to be set to increase, especially under the Social Dimension of Development (SDD) framework adopted by the government of Kenya. This is a strategy devised to cushion the poor against likely adverse effects of structural adjustment reforms. It comprises six broad generic areas of poverty-focused investments, aimed at enhancing the productive capacity of the poor to facilitate their integration into the market as well as providing a social safety net for those unable to adjust immediately to the market economy. Although largely a government initiative, designed to be implemented within the framework of the government's district focus for Rural Development, its conceptual framework identifies NGOs as key actors. Under the SDD programme, NGOs are expected to provide advisory skills to the government and private sector and to act as watchdogs on behalf of the community. They are also expected to act as channels through which other agencies link and interact with local grass-roots communities.

While a general inclination towards working with and funding NGOs directly is evident, not all NGOs have benefited from increased access to funding. Support to NGOs has been dependent on the degree of compliance with donor interests. The major recipients of direct funding have been those NGOs who demonstrated the ability to deliver effectively and efficiently in accordance with donor requirements, and who have the capacity to absorb the large amounts of money available through official aid. The majority of these NGOs, with the notable exception of a number of small and medium-sized professional organisations in the fields of democracy, governance and human rights, have been the larger NGOs, who already have a proven track record of competence in service delivery, managerial and financial skills. The majority of NGOs that have been considered eligible have been overseas NGOs. USAID and DFID have largely directed their support to such NGOs. The smaller bilateral donors such as SIDA, DANIDA and CIDA have been inclined towards operating within the existing government superstructure. This involves funding smaller NGOs and CBOs, and employing government staff at the district and divisional levels. The larger NGOs, have provided advisory services in the identification, appraisal, implementation, monitoring and evaluation of community-level projects.

---

[2] In 1995 total ODA flows to Kenya amounted to US$707 million, whereas in 1992 they were US$886 million (OECD 1996a).

Chapter 5

Changing Relationships in the South

The pace and the form which the direct funding mechanism took was influenced by the nature of the international aid climate at the time of its introduction and by differing national political climates. These common themes are the focus of this chapter, in which the impact of direct funding on southern NGOs and their position in the aid chain is reconsidered. The subsequent chapter will examine the implications of changes for northern NGOs and official agencies, draw together in summary the findings of the study and highlight those issues for management which emerge.

The three case studies provide different examples of how relationships between governments and southern NGOs have evolved under the particular pressures engendered by direct funding. In Bangladesh, funding to NGOs was a response to government incapacity in a situation of crisis. There was a subsequent attempt by government to control the growing influence of the NGO sector and impose restrictions on how and when foreign funds were used. Direct funding in the form of World Bank and USAID-sponsored social funds was channelled into Peru to bolster a government facing the twin challenges of guerrilla insurgency and a thriving drug economy. NGOs and their projects were adopted as a means of undermining the political appeal of the guerrilla movement and the economic inducements of the drug trade. In the case of Kenya, donors decided to work with NGOs as a means of bringing pressure to bear on the Moi government to institute genuine multiparty democracy. The government response to what it saw as a foreign-sponsored threat was a policy of intimidation and co-option aimed at weakening the NGO sector as a basis for opposition.

DIRECT FUNDING IN CONTEXT

The case studies illustrate that there have been profound changes in the roles and nature of the NGO sector (including both southern and northern NGOs) since the 1980s, as well as profound changes in the nature of the relationships between each of the traditional 'players' in development (the state, the official aid agencies, northern NGOs and southern NGOs). While these changes have been associated with the increasing use of direct funding as an instrument of aid, not all the changes can be attributed to its use alone: direct funding was introduced in the context of major shifts in both the political economy of aid and in official policies about aid that emerged after the debt crisis of the 1980s.

The 1980s and 1990s have been characterised by striking changes in the role of the state, and a growth in the role of northern governments in determining, through their respective aid agencies, the direction and purpose of development. With greater funds being directed towards the NGO sector and away from the state, tensions between them have been inevitable. While the role of NGOs in development has grown, their capacity to influence the 'development agenda' has been reduced by the way in which funding has been made available. Ideologies, value systems and aspirations have changed as they face the pressure to conform to standards and to perform according to procedures defined by the aid agencies. Funding for the NGO sector in the South has not been made universally accessible to all NGOs, but mainly to those whom the official aid agencies believe to be fulfilling what they think should be 'good' for the country.

The nature of funding has increasingly shifted away from the provision of grants for activities and ideas developed by NGOs, to the tendering for contracts to NGOs who are willing to deliver services that aid agencies wish to have provided. The result has been that the shape of the sector has been profoundly distorted, with a rapid growth of NGOs whose purpose is to deliver such services as are required by aid agencies. The effects have not been confined to southern NGOs alone. Perhaps the most disturbing effect of direct funding has been to transform the role of northern NGOs from being partners working in solidarity with the South to being either intermediaries in the subcontracting chain or becoming themselves direct competitors against southern NGOs for funds, and frequently the favoured partners of the aid agencies. Most aid agencies have argued that one of the main reasons for providing direct funding has been to strengthen civil society. The evidence from this study suggests that the shape and nature of civil society has been grossly deformed as a result of the selective funding of particular types of NGO activity.

Box 5.1: Campfire Association (Zimbabwe) and USAID

The Campfire Association has received US$1.8 million for a project in environment and tourism (1996–9), and an additional US$6 million for the Campfire Development Fund intended for Rural District Councils. A project manager was appointed by USAID to handle the administration of the grant. This was thought necessary because of the inadequate capacity of the NGO to deal with the complex reporting procedures required by USAID (the agency has thirty-two handbooks covering regulations for managing funds). The recruitment of the project manager was undertaken through an open tender and was eventually awarded to Development Associates, a US firm, Price Waterhouse in Zimbabwe was appointed as their local counterpart.

The funds for the project are all disbursed via the project manager, Development Associates, to the local NGO. A small amount for incidental expenses such as fuel and office consumables is disbursed upon request from the counterpart. The project management team is accountable only to USAID and not to the local NGO. The project manager is considered by USAID to have been put in place to protect, in the first instance, its own interests. Because it took time to complete the planning for the project and have all agreements in place, USAID provided a 'bridge grant' to supply limited funds for the project as an interim measure. New offices have been built to accommodate the team members next to the Campfire office. Besides managing the project fund, the project management team has also introduced new management systems for the NGO as a whole. Each of the project management team members has been appointed a counterpart in Campfire to train. USAID expected that, once trained, the management of funds would gradually be handed over from the Campfire Development Fund to Campfire staff. Advances on funds have been based on quarterly cash projections prepared by Campfire staff, subject to the approval of Development Associates. Project management overhead costs have been estimated to amount to 25% of the total budget.

There are concerns among local staff that the NGO may be losing its sense of identity as the project management team moves in and takes over the administration of the organisation completely. The NGO's management and staff have felt relegated to the role of implementing activities planned by others. Although hand over to local staff was intended, no schedule had been set for it. Many believe that USAID's approach has been patronising and has failed to recognise or make use of existing management capacity and local skills.

CASE STUDIES IN COMPARATIVE ANALYSIS

To understand the effect that the combination of aid policies and direct funding has had on the NGO sector, a distinction needs to be made between the form that direct funding took during the 1970s (i.e. in Bangladesh) and its form in the 1980s when it became so closely intertwined with the new neo-liberal policies of aid and development. The original form that direct funding took in the 1970s was the provision of substantial funds to a small number of NGOs to enable them to 'scale up' successful small projects that they had launched on their own initiative. Such funding was provided to enable services to reach large sections of the population who had been affected by massive social, economic and political upheavals associated with the civil war and cyclones of the early 1970s. Funding was provided to NGOs not as a means of reducing the role of the state in the provision of social services, but rather because the state infrastructure itself had virtually collapsed. Apart from a small group of NGOs, no one had any clear strategy for alleviating the immense crisis that vast numbers of people in Bangladesh faced. These NGOs were therefore able to set the agenda for their development programmes. The funding that they were provided with was, of necessity, flexible, enabling them to invest some of it in institutional capacity-building and training programmes, and for developing new initiatives for the future.

This form of direct funding was qualitatively different to that which was made available to NGOs in the 1980s, tied as it was to predefined perceptions about development. Although by this time the small group of NGOs that had benefited from direct funding in the 1970s had now become large and influential and therefore able to resist the pressures (to some extent) of the new aid ideology, the smaller NGOs in Bangladesh were faced, like other NGOs elsewhere, with direct funding in the form of limited period grants with no provision for core funding or institutional capacity-building, and provided in the form of contracts to deliver services that the aid agencies believed were required.

The relationship between NGOs and the state in Peru differs significantly from that in Bangladesh in large measure due to the relative strength of the Fujimori government. Interestingly, the donor community and especially multi-lateral agencies, such as the World Bank, appear to have accepted the extraordinary powers assumed by Fujimori. As a result, though there continue to be numerous challenges to the authority of the regime, none of which appear to threaten the regime's stability. In the case of a very strong regime, NGO involvement in the 'social fund' initiative did not represent a challenge or threat to the stability of the government, given that the aim of the initiative was to mitigate the impact of structural adjustment programmes.

Of more interest, however, is the character of those NGOs now working with the state. Whereas Latin America as a whole and Peru in particular both have a tradition of NGOs as radical social movements (often at the forefront of opposition to dictatorial regimes) these are not the same NGOs who are now working closely with the state. The direct funding experiment in Peru is noteworthy because of the fact that it relied heavily on organisations whose entire existence and survival was dependent on working with local communities in order to access resources from FONCODES. In many respects, therefore, there was a subcontractor relationship between the state and NGOs in which the terms of the debate, and what was to be delivered, were set entirely by the state and the World Bank. NGOs were expected to compete with one another (and other CBOs) for contracts to implement small-scale projects in rural areas. Many of the tensions that have arisen in Bangladesh about the nature of state–NGO co-operation have not surfaced in Peru because the 'third-generation' Peruvian NGOs do not have the experience or the capacity to play anything other than a subordinate role to the state. In many respects, therefore, the social fund experiment has succeeded in creating a class of NGOs who are entirely under the sway of the government. Older NGOs, on the other hand, have found themselves in the development wilderness, bypassed by the government and a new set of partners from within civil society.

The emergence of government-sponsored NGOs, which has not been restricted to Peru, raises serious questions about the nature of civil society and commitment to good governance. NGOs everywhere have faced a difficult dilemma of wanting, on the one hand, to have access to the highest levels of policy-making in the country, and on the other to maintain their own organisational autonomy. Thus, for example, in Bangladesh NGOs have reacted with suspicion to overtures from the government. Indeed, in a meeting on government–NGO relations sponsored by the World Bank, the editor of one of Bangladesh's leading English dailies warned NGOs not to sacrifice their right to be critical of the government in order to gain access to national policy-making forums. While he welcomed the moves towards greater co-operation between NGOs and the government, he also cautioned against NGOs becoming too comfortable lest they end up losing those characteristics that made NGOs an attractive alternative to the state in the first place. In much the same way that the media has a responsibility to maintain its independence, so he felt, NGOs must guard against complacency and ensure their continued independence. In the case of Peru, however, it seems that one problem with the social fund experiment in its current form is that it has created an entire class of subcontractors in the shape of NGOs whose appearance and *raison d'être* are derived from the attraction of significant amounts of funds. What will happen to such NGOs when the supply of money dries up remains to be seen.

The relationship between the NGO sector and the state in Kenya has been fraught with difficulties and tensions. Colonialism in Kenya saw the emergence of numerous associations confronting and lobbying the colonial state on a wide-range of social, political and economic injustices to which the population was subjected. It also saw consistent attempts by the colonial state to undermine and constrict this indigenous civil associational life, as part of a broad strategy to consolidate its own domination. Many of these associations were therefore either proscribed or relegated to the district levels. However, they continued to organise and provided the nurturing ground for many of the pre- and post-independence activist and nationalist movements. The post-independence era saw two parallel developments in the state–civil society organisations relationship in Kenya. The state recognised the social and economic benefits derived from the work of such organisations, but at the same time sought to control and limit their role within certain parameters which the new regime defined as 'nation-building'. Thus while welfare and development NGOs were promoted and grew in numbers during the Kenyatta regime, civil organisations formally opposed to the regime's excesses and seeking social, economic and political reforms were enfeebled through co-option, reshaping or outright proscription.

This muzzling of civil associational life heightened with the proscription in 1969 of the Kenya People's Union (KPU), making Kenya a *de facto* one-party system. Following the increased repression in the aftermath of the failed coup attempt in 1982, there was a period of minimal overt challenges to the state's excesses. By 1985, however, growing incidences of political and human rights suppression, corruption and other forms of social abuses, prompted the church and professional bodies to focus on issues of social, economic and political justice, and to challenge the state for reforms. Meanwhile the international community had become displeased with the performance of the state and was keen to see an expanded non-state participation in socio-economic and political advancement and a more plural society. They were increasingly making more resources available to NGOs while diminishing the role of the state through reduced bilateral funding. This resulted in further growth within the NGO sector, with many organisations extending their scope to incorporate a democracy and governance agenda, and intensifying the pressure on the state for social, economic and political reforms.

The state for its part became increasingly concerned about its lack of access to and control over resources and the degree of power and autonomy available to civil institutions. Several attempts were made to control NGOs, including the former strategies of co-option and proscription. But, both as a result of growing international concern about the regime's repressive behaviour and because of the rising militancy of many NGOs, these attempts have been largely unsuccessful. On the contrary, the measures that the Moi regime sought to introduce to control NGOs led to a growing solidarity and closer networking and co-ordination within the NGO sector than has ever been seen before. Furthermore, the state was forced to recognise the NGOs' co-ordination body as a legitimate voice for the sector, and under pressure from sections of the official aid community, conceded to enter into negotiations over the terms of the new legislation introduced to control NGOs. With Moi's victory in the elections in 1997, it remains unclear whether the breathing space created by the NGOs through their confrontations with the state will remain open. Early signs provide little grounds for optimism.

ACCOUNTABILITY AND AGENDA SETTING

A central theme running through this discussion of state–NGO relations has been: Who sets the development agenda? This question concerns lack of co-ordination and co-operation between NGOs and their counterparts in the government. For the most part, be it in Bangladesh, Kenya or Peru, it seems clear that one of the main effects of direct funding has been to remove control of development policy from the hands of the state to the hands of those controlling the purse-strings, the official aid agencies. Where the creation of a model that seeks to bypass an inefficient or corrupt state (Bangladesh and Kenya) or to compensate for the shortcomings of the state (Peru) has had the impact of devolving some of the day-to-day management of development activities to individual NGOs, the real question has become the competence of the organisations involved and the legitimacy of this transfer.

Although in all three cases, the NGO sector has benefited from access to bilateral funds, the period during which they were able to access these funds differed dramatically and this had an impact on who set the agenda. In Bangladesh, it can be argued that NGOs were better rooted in the communities in which they worked, less reliant on northern NGOs and therefore in a stronger position to assume some of the responsibilities of agenda-setting, than their counterparts in Kenya and Peru. In both these countries, the level of development of the NGO sector was not as advanced as in Bangladesh when direct funding began. In Kenya, this has resulted in a two-tier programme in which northern NGOs have worked with local agencies to develop their capacity to work more closely with bilateral agencies. Here much of the agenda continued to be set by a combination of northern NGOs and bilateral donors and then 'exported' to local organisations who may or may not assume ownership. At this stage, it is hard to predict the impact of this change on the Kenyan NGO scene. However, if the experiences of Togo and Sri Lanka (Smillie 1995) are anything to go by, then there is a risk that direct funding could actually retard the ability of local organisations to develop their capacity to formulate policies independently of outside agencies. In the long run, the issue is whether or not the clear divisions drawn between NGOs and the state will come back to haunt the local NGO sector. That is to say, regardless of what may be thought about external agencies and their involvement in development activities, at some point NGOs will have to work with the state.

In the case of Kenya, however, direct funding may well have both weakened the capacities of local NGOs to work independently and created a permanent animus between the state bureaucracy and NGOs. In Peru, the situation is different. The main vehicle of funds for NGOs has been the World Bank supported FONCODES and Counterpart funds, where the aim has been to build support for the economic reform process by providing resources to NGOs and CBOs to implement projects aimed at easing the burden of structural adjustment programmes on the very poor. However, the World Bank has been very careful to specify the types of project to be funded. As a result, a situation arises where NGOs and community groups have been specifically created to take advantage of manufactured opportunities, regardless of whether or not this fell within their agenda. While in Bangladesh one could argue that there were demands for direct funding with the consequent enhancement in the sector, in Kenya and Peru the push in favour of NGOs was a supply-side event, driven by the availability of cheap resources.

Referring to Bangladesh, G. D. Wood (1994) argued that while working through NGOs has many advantages – not least allowing the poor some semblance of participation in decision-making, as well as providing coverage to those who fall beyond the main government programmes – this has to be weighed against the negative impact on governance. He argued that in most Western societies, the government is ultimately responsible for the provision of services and the fulfilment of that responsibility is judged by the electorate. However, if the responsibility for providing services falls on NGOs, the equation changes considerably. Most NGOs in the three countries examined here were not membership organisations, and had, therefore, few formal mechanisms to hold them accountable to their constituencies or beneficiaries. Wood pointed out that given the absence of formal accountability methods within local NGOs, beneficiaries do not have any means of redress other than leaving the group. Under such circumstances, the government is effectively absolved from any responsibility of ensuring that basic services arc provided. The net result is a situation where the government is no longer accountable to its citizens.

This raises the question of whether or not it is possible to reconcile a desire to improve the delivery of services to the poor with efforts to support the development of a pluralistic and strong civil society. As Riddell and Bebbington (1995) have pointed out, it is by no means guaranteed that a policy which aims to improve service delivery through NGOs will at the same time strengthen civil society and increase the transparency and accountability of the government. In fact, as the case studies have shown, direct funding has more often than not had a detrimental impact on the relationship between the sector and the state. One accusation has been that the efforts to work through NGOs have been a part of the ongoing battle against big government. However, rather than the desired improvement in the quality of services, we have seen a situation where the government's capacity to act and implement policies is severely reduced. Rather than leading to an overall improvement in the welfare of the poor, there has been what Shillelagh Stewart describes as 'capacity shuffling' (1997). Writing about South Africa, she argues that there is no real net gain in social welfare as a result of working through NGOs, but simply a redistribution of resources and expertise to the NGO sector. She questions whether or not this arrangement can be justified from anything other than an ideological standpoint.

Their right to play a part in setting the development agenda is a question of independence for NGOs. It is closely tied to the conceptualisation of civil society in which organisations including NGOs and CBOs are able to provide a check and balance to the state through their supposed proximity to constituencies and autonomy to represent their interests. At the root of independence is the issue of access to resources. The donor community claims to be promoting the role of southern NGOs in the good governance agenda using the mechanism of direct funding. However, experiences from the South both expose the complexities of this notion and raise questions for northern NGOs and official agencies about the nature of their relationship with southern NGOs and about the management of direct funding.

Chapter 6

Implications of Direct Funding

This study has shown that there is a broad spectrum of experience of direct funding among all the key players. With increases in incidence and volume, direct funding has placed actors under specific pressures, which have contributed to a culture shift in the development environment. Northern NGOs have been making strategic choices related to changes in availability of funding, with crucial implications both for individual organisations and for the evolution of the sector as a whole. This chapter exposes those choices in the light of their implications for the practice of development by the sector. In the evaluation of the impact of direct funding it is necessary to define the benchmark of good practice against an open acknowledgement of purpose. The key issue for NGOs is whether in the use of direct funding they are working towards the efficient delivery of aid at the expense of their commitment to poverty alleviation. Simply put, have the relationships wrought by the direct funding mechanism shifted NGO accountability decisively away from community and target groups towards official agencies?

DIRECT FUNDING AND NORTHERN NGOS

Without doubt, the increase in direct funding by northern-based donors to southern NGOs has significantly challenged northern NGOs to reconsider their position. Many of these agencies had assumed that a near monopoly of contact with southern NGOs was their prerogative. What we now see is a regrouping of the northern NGO sector, as individual organisations seek to re-establish their roles and revise their *raison d'être*. We witness three major and sometimes contradictory trends.

First, many of the northern NGOs which provide financial support for southern NGOs (rather than implement projects themselves) have fought internally about how to be good donors. For some this has meant increasing the number of indigenous staff and decentralising operations. Others have sought to re-establish a field presence in order to be closer to their southern NGO partners.[1] For example, many of the church-based agencies which hitherto relied on local churches as their natural partners, have pushed staff out into new field offices in order to demonstrate close contacts with partners and counteract charges that they fail to illustrate any comparative advantage over locally based official agency staff.

A second and significantly large group has chosen to become contractors for northern official agencies. Thus certain agencies, such as CARE, have grown on the back of contracts for major official donors.[2] As an adjunct to the contracting mode we also see several agencies absorbing a considerable proportion of the increased funds available for emergency work on a contractual or semi-contractual basis. Ironically some of those agencies assuming contracts for emergencies are donors who are simultaneously trying to decentralise and indigenise their development operations.

The third group are fortunate enough in their own terms to be able to ignore the other current trends working against the traditional northern NGOs because of the continued popularity with the donor public of child sponsorship. Agencies such as Plan International have continued to grow through child sponsorship, despite serious doubts surrounding the effectiveness of child sponsorship developmentally and increasing criticism of the approach amongst professional development workers (Smillie 1998).

It would be wrong to think that all northern NGOs could be fitted into one or another of these groups: some organisations have adopted a combination of these. However, adopting a selection of measures which in practice may be contradictory has created tensions. Consequently, many agencies have been engaged in difficult internal debates in an attempt (most frequently failed) to resolve contradictions. The 1990s have been characterised by uncertainty within northern NGOs. Almost endemic internal crisis is illustrated by regular restructuring and the instability of top management (shown through rapid turnover of northern NGO directors and difficulties recruiting for senior positions).

As southern NGOs increased their influence over developmental activities in their own countries, often supported directly by northern official agencies, many official donors directly challenged the northern NGOs to show their worth in the development chain. Official agencies wanted NGOs to demonstrate comparative advantage as a channel of funds, in terms of the value they can add

---

[1] See forthcoming INTRAC Occasional Paper on decentralisation.

[2] Smillie (unpublished) describes the following as 'super NGOs': World Vision, Oxfam, Care, Plan International and Save the Children. They are characterised by a network of organisations based in the North, each with a budget in excess (some well in excess) of US$10 million in 1995.

to the development process. Northern NGOs responded in several ways but their strongest defences often related to the longer-term perspective of many northern NGOs, who could show continuous support for partners often over decades. Others spoke in general terms of the importance of solidarity or partnership only to find that these concepts in turn were questioned and dissected by official agencies, and even sometimes by southern partners themselves. One of the ironies revealed by this research is that although northern NGOs have been trying since their inception to build the capacity of southern NGOs through partnership, it is in Bangladesh where we find a robust sector, and in that case study the southern NGOs built capacity themselves.

In order to justify the value of their role to official agencies, northern NGOs sought to fashion themselves as one of the following:

- a net contributor of funds and/or other measurable resources;
- involved in advocacy and policy development; and
- a provider of technical expertise.

Many northern NGOs have become channels for the funds of their home governments. It has been difficult for some northern NGO donors in this position to justify why this should continue to be the case. Other NGOs work with funds raised from a mix of sources, including their own fund-raising efforts with the public and government funds. Such organisations can argue equally forcefully that they are net providers of resources. Those who deal only in government funds could be classified as contractors, managing funds for government rather than providing services on contract.

Such agencies feel that accumulated experience as a donor has enabled them to provide a service of better quality in comparison with some of the newer funding practices coming out of official agencies. In this instance there is considerable pressure on such NGOs to prove their case. Much of the evidence, which has to come from southern partners or recipients of funds channelled in this way, is not as positive as many northern NGOs would hope. It is worth adding here that where official agencies have reduced funds to northern NGOs (because they have not been convinced by the arguments in favour of pushing their resources through such channels) those northern NGOs which do have their own publicly raised resources have survived cuts far better than those without their own funds. This is not only because of the obvious reason that they were less dependent, but also because they could demonstrate a degree of public support for their activities.[3] Furthermore, by generating funds autonomously, NGOs have been able to access 'matching funds' from official

---

[3] See Smillie, (1996), 'Canada: A Cautionary Tale', in Smillie.et al.

agencies. For example, 63 out of 95 named British NGOs which received funding from DFID in 1996/7 did so through the Joint Funding Scheme, which accounts for 24% of DFID expenditure through British NGOs (DFID 1997).

The second area worth further exploration is advocacy. Many northern NGOs at least pay lip-service to the importance of advocacy. It is difficult to argue that the 1990s have been a period in which development northern NGOs have captured the public imagination. There seems to have been a decline in public interest in the great issues and it is not evident that northern NGOs have been fully engaged in attempts to reverse this. The campaigning political space has, however, been filled by NGOs campaigning on environmental and human rights issues. These organisations have not necessarily been involved in the transfer of financial resources. Uncertainty over independent financial resources has led many northern NGOs to reduce rather than increase their campaigning, lobbying, advocacy and policy activities.[4] Some agencies would argue that they have moved away from high profile, public campaigning towards more focused individual and targeted lobbying. Our interviews with official agencies have not, however, always shown that they would concur with this perception.

A further concern is that southern NGOs are not always convinced that advocacy work in the North reflects the priorities of the South. Southern concerns are not always of sufficient immediate relevance to public interest to be realistically taken up in the North, or they may not arise at a time which suits the timetable of debate adhered to by some of the larger multinational agencies, for example. However, there is sometimes a concern that northern NGOs are compromised in a conflict of interest between the positions taken by their own donors and issues raised by their partners in the South. Examples of this include the unwillingness of the NGO sector to tackle the EC over the quality of aid, and recent tensions between Nordic governments and child rights agencies over the Convention on Child Labour. In recent years, networks and initiatives from the South have sought to address this perceived gap between their own concerns and those of northern-based agencies. Some such networks include Focus on the Global South, the International Consumers' Union and southern groups in the World Bank NGO committee. The challenge now being picked up by some northern NGOs is how to campaign as much as possible on an advocacy agenda which is genuinely agreed with their southern partners. Some northern NGOs are devoting significant resources to this aspect of their work.

In the third area, as providers of technical expertise some northern NGOs seem to be hostages to their own history. Many volunteer- and other personnel-sending agencies were established on the basis that development was hindered by shortages of skills in countries of the South. Subsequently, in many countries the need for external human resources was reduced significantly. It is growing increasingly difficult to justify the employment of expatriate technical officers. Indeed, there are notable cases where southern countries have exported their own surplus skills. For example, India provides a significant number of UN staff. UN volunteers are now predominantly from the South, such that the programme represents a far more successful South to South operation than any volunteer-sending northern NGO. In addition to a situation in which fewer countries genuinely have an overall skill shortage which can be met from outside, the level of those skills required and requested is now far higher than even a decade ago. As local staff fill positions there has been an inflation in the qualifications and skills still required. Thus the real need is for fewer and better-qualified expatriate personnel, and for staff with qualitatively different skills than those employed in the past: skills, for example, in institutional strengthening and capacity-building rather than technical know-how. The expatriate development workers of the present are not required 'to do' so much as to facilitate the activity of others.

The terms on which funding is granted to northern NGOs is crucial to their independence and legitimacy. Even in the context of a traditionally supportive government apparatus many Canadian NGOs were closed in consequence of the draconian cuts in Canadian assistance in 1989 (Smillie et al. 1996). Although they are reluctant to acknowledge it, the fates of individual European NGOs can be hostage to change in official policy. Shifts in funding trends such as moving towards using northern NGOs as channels for funding, or choosing between northern NGOs, southern NGOs and even private firms when granting contracts, are issues of policy which threaten the nature and existence of NGOs. Money or resources which come without strings attached are usually generated by the NGO itself, either through public giving, trading and other economic activities or existing endowments. These core funds allow an NGO to make independent decisions on where to work, whom to support and whether to get involved in development education, advocacy and research. As roles are forced to change through both financial pressures and a recognition that southern NGOs can and should replace northern NGOs in many areas, those NGOs in the North which can depend on access to money on their own terms are most likely to survive and flourish.

Of equal importance, however, is the need for northern NGOs to make informed strategic choices about their evolution in response to a changing funding environment. If northern NGOs are in effect transforming their organisa-

---

[4] For example, spending on development education by NGOs in the North has been slashed as funding to northern NGOs has declined (see Randel and German 1996).

tional format in order to access funds locally then they should recognise that they are entering into a competitive relationship with southern NGOs. Similarly, if northern NGOs take a role as donors *vis-à-vis* southern NGOs this choice has implications. Northern NGOs need to be open about whether, by acting as donors in support of particular initiatives, their primary aim is to work in solidarity with their southern counterparts or to serve government agencies in their promotion of a political agenda. Without this transparency the rhetoric of partnership will seduce organisations into relationships which can damage not only themselves but also contribute to the weakening of the sector as a whole.

PARTNERSHIP

Related to (but not synonymous with) the issue of access to funds is that of the social legitimacy of NGOs (both northern or southern), and in particular whether they have a local constituency. Some of the pressure from donors on northern NGOs to prove their worth has been mitigated by the ability to demonstrate support from a local constituency. This support may be in the form of funds but also through reinforcing advocacy messages. Since the late 1980s, the environmental lobby has been more successful than development NGOs at promoting popular support for their cause and developing membership bases. However, in recent years several northern NGOs have recognised the importance of a solid membership and have sought to create or resurrect one. It could be argued that the legitimacy of northern NGOs is weakened by relatively easy access to official funds, which undermines the strict necessity of undertaking the slow, hard work of developing public interest and support. Southern NGOs should look to the recent history of their northern counterparts in this respect, as, without a support base in the public, many of them are equally vulnerable.

It became clear early in this study that there was a major difference in perception over the concept of partnership between NGOs in the South and the North. Whilst northerners espoused the rhetoric of partnership and claimed that strong partnerships distinguished them from official agencies, the same view was not always held by their partners in the South. Complacency on the part of northern NGOs or failure to acknowledge inequality in the relationship between donor and recipient were not foundations for a relationship that could withstand the advances of official donors, who have displaced northern NGOs in their relationships with southern NGOs. If the rhetoric of partnership is to be translated into an equitable relationship, it probably implies a greater degree of balance between the power of northern and southern actors. The funding relationship will always make this difficult, but not impossible. The challenge for many northern NGOs is to recognise this difficulty rather than to deny or ignore it. If they fail to grasp the need to base the quality of their relationships on something more than financial ties, then they can expect to be supplanted if other sources of funding become available.

Although it is sometimes hard for northern NGOs to accept, our study showed that many southern NGOs make scant distinction between funds received from official agencies and northern NGOs. Across the country studies this conclusion was consistent. Certain elements in a funding relationship were considered more important than the status of the donor organisation. For example, the presence of an office locally (be it attached to an embassy or an NGO field office) was considered to be important. Southern NGOs like to know who they are dealing with and to have constant access to contacts in donor organisations rather than receive occasional flying visits. If an official in an embassy is accessible this is considered to be worth more than the rhetoric of partnership from an NGO at a distance (Muchunguzi and Milne n.d.).

It is recognised that official funds are not without their problems. Those countries and areas which have suffered from changes in policy and/or reductions in government budgets were aware that official policies could often be very short term. This reinforces the argument made by some northern NGOs, that their value lies in long-term accompaniment rather than short-term funding of southern NGOs. It was also recognised that not all official agencies were the same, there were marked differences in philosophies, levels of flexibility and conditionality, strictness of procedures and the basic capacity to manage programmes.

In some areas (e.g. Peru) it was recognised that northern NGOs were more likely to support democratic development or civil society types of programme than official agencies. Despite the rhetoric which has in recent years supported civil society, many southern NGOs did not find that reality measured up to promises. The case study of Peru demonstrated this difference most clearly between the two types of donor, with northern NGOs being the mainstay of the more critical, research-based programmes, and official funds being short term and semi-contractual in nature.

The perception of many people in the southern NGO sector is that northern NGOs feel threatened by direct funding. This makes them cautious to heed warnings from northern NGOs about the dangers or pitfalls inherent in becoming dependent upon official funds. They point to northern NGOs' own dependence on official funds, and argue that it is hypocritical of them to condemn the relationship. It can easily appear that northern NGOs are motivated by either paternalism (taking the attitude that southern NGOs are not able to make informed judgements themselves) or self-interest in their criticism of direct funding. Mistrust of northern NGOs in this respect is underpinned by the activities of northern NGOs who have sought to access the direct funding pot, through either posing as local NGOs or utilising their field operations to secure eligibility for such funds and contracts.

Box 6.1: Rejection of Direct Funding

A number of Zimbabwean NGOs claim to have rejected offers of direct funding either because of the conditions attached to grants or because of fears about the effect such grants might have on their organisations. CADEC had, for example, been offered funds from DFID for work in Matebeleland, but had opted instead to have funds channelled through UK-based NGOs. CADEC stated that they preferred this route because they already knew the people involved in the northern NGOs, and they were often able to obtain advance funding in a way that would not have been possible with the official agencies.

At the end of the day many southern NGOs will try to maintain a mixture of NGO and official funds in an effort to maximise the respective advantages of both. As many of them argue, official funds take longer to approve but once they arrive the quantity is larger. Thus the ratio of effort to benefits is greater than it is when dealing with a myriad of smaller northern NGO donors. Unfortunately the procedures and conditionalities imposed by northern NGOs are often no less onerous than those of official funders. Northern NGOs seem increasingly to be obliged to pass donors' conditionalities on to their southern NGO partners. These partners are then faced with two sets of conditions in a differentiated funding chain: from the official donor and the northern NGO.

One of the effects of direct funding on the NGO environment in southern countries has been to place immense pressure on southern NGOs to break with their constituencies in the process of becoming accountable primarily to their donors (regardless of whether they are NGOs or official agencies). Although described differently, what comes out of each case study is the birth and flourishment of a new sector of NGOs whose primary purpose is to feed on a sub-contracting culture and who are crowding out the sector and contributing to a fundamental shift in culture. This raises the question of whether at the current time development is predominantly an activity whose focus is needs based, or whether the balance has tipped to such a degree that the emphasis is now on the efficient delivery of aid. A shift in the direction of accountability away from grass-roots constituencies is both cause and consequence of this as NGOs have come under pressure from official donors to absorb funding tied to service delivery.

SUMMARY OF MAIN FINDINGS

In summary, some of the findings of this study on the impact of direct funding on the NGO sector, and its effect on civil society are that:

1. A considerable amount of money is now available to NGOs and CBOs through different official funding mechanisms. In some of the countries studied official donors are now the main source of support to local NGOs.

2. There is a general tendency to underestimate the total official funds available. The majority of funds do not come from the traditional NGO units of official agencies in headquarters, but through bilateral programmes, as either grants or contracts. Since these funds are not distinguished clearly, it is only by looking at the funds available in a specific country (as in the case studies) that one can begin to appreciate quite how important official direct funding now is for local NGOs.

3. It is also clear that despite the policy of providing support to civil society in a general sense, many of the available funds are dedicated to specific sectoral and service delivery objectives. Furthermore, the funds are delivered through contractual mechanisms. We cannot talk about partnership in those cases where strict contractual forms are followed and the southern NGO is merely providing services according to a binding contract. It is difficult to see how such contracting strengthens civil society. Indeed, there is some evidence that it might weaken it: on the one hand by failing to take into account the need for government to be of sufficient strength to operate and maintain a stable democratic regime. On the other hand by focusing on NGOs as contractors and endowing them with resources at the expense of other civil society organisations, direct funding may be simultaneously pulling civil society in opposite directions.

4. As is indeed the case in the North, some southern NGOs owe their existence to official funds. The supply of funds and the demand for suitable partners has stimulated massive growth in the number of NGOs in many parts of the world. The question in many countries now is how sustainable in the longer term this growth of organisations can be: hence an upsurge in interest in local philanthropy and self-generated income sources for NGOs.

5. This study uncovered a discernible tendency for some official agencies to move towards direct funding of CBOs. The logic behind this lies in a desire to ensure that assistance is concentrated as closely as possible to the ultimate beneficiaries. Bypassing yet another intermediate level, this shift represents the logic behind direct funding of southern NGOs taken to a further extreme. Concern for the sustainability of CBOs is even greater than for southern NGOs, as is the cost of an official agency trying to deliver services directly to communities. We also uncovered examples where an official agency claimed to be pro-

viding support directly to communities at no or very low costs, but where in actual fact NGOs were absorbing the real costs themselves.[5] Thus an NGO would prepare all the plans and technical studies for sinking a community well or building a local school, and the official donor would provide the construction costs to the community, claiming success in the provision of a service without intermediate support. In reality the NGO subsidises the official donor and pays for the costs of delivery using its own resources.

6. Despite the attractiveness of accessing official funds in order to increase scale, the study showed that even relatively big southern NGOs faced problems in servicing larger grants. Similarly, many encountered serious constraints to scaling up their organisational capacity in order to absorb higher levels of income. Some failed to meet this challenge. Few official agencies, in administering funding, took the organisational and other costs of scaling up into account.

7. It is still the case that a great deal of direct funding is available only for very short-term project-based activities. Few official agencies have designed longer-term, core funding for southern NGO programme work.

8. Thus an increasing number of southern NGOs are now gaining access to official funds and for larger amounts than they previously received from northern NGOs. However, if the case of Bangladesh were to be repeated elsewhere we might see a situation in which an increasing proportion of funding is channelled to a smaller number of large NGOs which have a track record of dealing with large-scale programmes.

There is still a question which hangs over this debate and which relates to the future. If the practice of direct funding by official agencies should be reversed the future for southern NGOs would be uncertain. It is possible that the autonomy of those northern NGOs who have acted primarily as donors may be irrevocably undermined in their capacity to support southern NGOs. There is no reason to assume that these organisations could or would re-emerge to fill any gap left by official donors. It could be that as a result of direct funding and in the event that official funds were removed, the northern NGO sector will have diminished in size and strength and its links with southern NGOs weakened beyond repair. It is true that interest in alternative fund-raising (including philanthropy and income-generating schemes) has grown, but it is questionable whether these alternatives (still minuscule compared to other income streams for the NGO sector globally) could really consolidate the difference. NGOs were initially envisaged as a short-term historical phenomena which would eventually work themselves out of existence. Some would argue therefore that

---

[5] Unpublished research by B. Pratt and S. Matsvai in Zimbabwe.

direct funding was working to precipitate a state of affairs in which the NGO sector as a whole was composed of a domestic welfare sector (primarily including organisations of a size which can be supported by the domestic economy and local philanthropy in the South), complemented by lobbying and interest groups, much as one would find in most developed countries.

THE MANAGEMENT OF DIRECT FUNDING: IMPLICATIONS FOR OFFICIAL DONORS

Many of the studies of direct funding although mostly commissioned by official agencies have not dealt with the implications for the commissioning agencies themselves. In general, however, official agencies have underestimated the requirements of small scale funding of NGOs compared with traditional large bilateral government-to-government programmes. Furthermore, official agencies have assumed that their own ways of working, moulded by years of civil service practice, are immune to lessons which can be learnt from working in very different environments.

In reviewing the direct funding policies of official agencies, the lack of a coherent strategy becomes clear. On one level, no single strategy concerning direct funding exists agency-wide, thus the NGO unit may be working from a perspective not shared by the bilateral desk of a major donor. This may facilitate a positive flexibility in the system, but equally it could prevent consistency in the motivation to support NGO work and how it should best be supported. The differences within agencies also make it difficult to answer the question of whether direct funding assists partnership and the development of civil society or alternatively merely promotes the growth of a contract culture. The truth in many official agencies is probably yes and no, to both, given that contradictory policies may be pursued by different parts of the same agency. At the level of individual projects, objectives may become more clearly identifiable, but the evidence does not always confirm this either.

Once they have addressed the need to formulate a strategy and establish goals in relation to the direct funding mechanism, and in addition to fielding political objections from their home NGO community, official agencies seem to encounter problems managing direct funding in practice. Certain problems can be traced to the major differences between funding government programmes and NGOs. These differences impact on everything from procedures to the human resources required to manage the programmes.

Many procedures employed in the management of direct funding are inflexible and more appropriate to a different type of development. Rigid interpretation of the logical framework analysis is illustrative of a focus on activities and

95

outputs by many official agencies, which sits uncomfortably with process-oriented projects based in turbulent, unstable or poor communities. Accountancy rules seemed to be designed for programmes far bigger than even the largest NGOs generally manage and are often dominated, even obsessed by, procurement rules and asset management.

One of the most common problems in the administration of direct funding, which has been transplanted from negotiation processes designed for bilateral programmes, is the long lead time. An excessive length of time is characteristically spent on the early stages of a programme, at design and appraisal, in comparison with the relatively little time devoted to monitoring and evaluation. Most in-country funding programmes examined by this research had experienced little in the way of monitoring and evaluation (except that already done by the recipients themselves). This has significantly reduced the capacity of the donor agency staff to learn. It also indicates a lack of understanding of the value of amendments and changes to a programme, which results from the process of engagement and implementation. It is a familiar concept to NGOs that a programme will develop through time and with the learning engendered by trial and error, but this is a process which demands monitoring and evaluation of reactions to external and internal variables and, most importantly, the evolving needs and understanding of the prime stakeholders. However, this approach is prohibited by a system rooted in mutual mistrust, between government agencies concerned either to obtain maximum benefit from assistance or to ensure the maximum number of controls to avoid misuse or redirection of funds by organisations in the South managing the responsibility of implementating programmes.

Lack of good monitoring and evaluation practices by official agencies also reduces the degree of impact of certain types of funding. The proliferation of micro-grants from some agencies has occurred in a context where little can be done to show conclusively whether these grants actually have any positive impact on their recipients, CBOs. Examples include micro-grants administered by the EU and by the Canada Fund in Peru. Such large grant-funding bodies conduct virtually no follow-up once the grants have been made. It is therefore not surprising that it is difficult to comment on the impact of such grants, or that the grant-giving staff were basing their funding decisions on little more than assumptions and pious hope.

The time and human resources required to manage NGO programmes seems greater than traditional programmes. Major agencies admitted, in the process of this research, that they are often constrained in the management of the programmes, direct funding because they have underestimated the time programmes will absorb and consequently do not have adequate human resources to service the projects. For an official agency planning to work with NGOs it is crucial to assess capacity to resource the programme sufficiently. The human resources required include local or long-term expatriate staff who can bring both local knowledge and an understanding of how NGOs work. Some agencies now recognise that because NGOs do work in ways that are different from government different specialist staff are required to advise on or manage co-operation.

Current determination to ensure direct delivery of assistance and services via an intermediary, whether NGO or CBO, has meant that resources for capacity-building have not always been allocated in a manner designed to improve local capacities. Among some of the southern NGOs we studied it became clear that northern NGOs were providing the resources to build and maintain capacities which could then be used to deliver services on behalf of official agencies (Smillie 1998). Certain official agency personnel still seem to believe that the capacity of NGOs to deliver services evolves through a spontaneous process, divorced from economic realities, human resource capacity or organisational development programmes. They are then surprised when their plans to deliver small credit or primary health care packages, for example, are frustrated by the lack of organisational and human resources to manage the delivery of these programmes. Recent work in the Commonwealth of Independent States (CIS) has revealed this lack of understanding by many official agencies to be bordering on the professionally incompetent. Official agencies were found to aggressively promote their favoured programmes without due regard to local capacity-building needs. Ultimately it is these needs which have to be met in order to provide the frameworks to deliver these or other services.

On a more positive note there is some evidence that official agencies are beginning to reconsider their ways of working as a result of exposure to NGOs. Methods such as PRA, for example, have come to challenge the classic approach to identifying needs at community level employed by consultants and government officials. A new awareness of the importance of concepts such as partnership, participation, primary stakeholding, poverty focus and others can be found in many official agencies. However, this rhetoric of learning and fruitful interaction with the NGO sector in the South can be meaningful only in practice where it is matched by a funding strategy which permits learning, where the mechanisms chosen to operationalise policy are appropriate to the task in hand and where the resources required are available to ensure the programme is managed well.

Postscript

It has not been easy to draw conclusions in a sector characterised by rapid change or to define a series of complex issues around civil society and relationships between different institutional actors. One could not pretend that these relationships are anything but fluid, and even concepts such as 'contracting' may differ greatly between different partners. We do feel, however, that this study has provided some clarity on the problems surrounding direct funding and the sometimes contradictory policies being pursued by the major agencies: contradictions which may undermine the goals of programmes being supported by these agencies.

A great deal has changed since we first started to look at the increasing proportion of funding being directed at southern (and now eastern) NGOs by official agencies. If we look to the future there is little reason to expect any major change in this trend. Official agencies have strengthened their capacity to support such funding programmes, northern NGOs are still trying to adapt to the implications for their own roles. There are new and related debates emerging, however. The subtle change in emphasis from NGOs to civil society organisations may well herald further developments. As official agencies explore and experiment with funds to organisations other than 'traditional NGOs', we may see increased funds for community-based and membership organisations (including trade unions, chambers of commerce or professional associations) precipitate a challenge to the present role played by southern NGOs.

As this study shows, the attempt to support civil society through funding southern NGOs has sometimes backfired. One reason why NGOs were originally identified as desirable partners was because of their perceived proximity to the poor. However, NGOs have inevitably been alienated from their constituencies by the pull of accountability upwards. The result has been the creation of a set of institutions no longer accountable to the poor and a class of professionals dependent on the continued existence of these southern NGOs. Perhaps it is no surprise that donors are now looking beyond NGOs to find alternatives which fit their original image of organisations rooted in the community.

There is also some indication that major agencies as diverse as the World Bank and DFID are 'rediscovering the state', demonstrating awareness that support for NGOs does not replace the role of the state in crucial areas, such as basic health and education services. Therefore, we may see a move back towards partnership with the state in some sectors, in recognition that in some areas NGOs are now playing too large a role and should curb their activities to a level consistent with a supplementary or supportive purpose. The often quoted issue of sustainability is also being raised, as official donors become increasingly concerned about the longer-term sustainability of a system dependent upon foreign funding of basic services via local NGOs. The absence of clear alternative sources of funding in many countries, especially the poorer, is leading official agencies to question the wisdom of promoting a scale of service delivery, such as seen in Bangladesh, which could not be sustained by the local economy. The longer-term role of the state as supporting services through the tax base therefore becomes more attractive to donors concerned lest they become tied to servicing recurrent, long-term costs. The reaction to this possibility is an enhanced interest in income-generating schemes and local philanthropy to provide new sources of funds for southern NGOs.

In our own work we will continue to monitor these and other changing patterns as relationships develop and new institutional forms emerge which may further challenge the perceptions and prejudices of the development community.

Appendix I

Research Methodology

The research focused on four main areas:

- the dynamics of funding from official sources to northern NGOs;
- the consequences of greater interaction on the development policies and practices of both parties;
- the phenomenon of direct support by official agencies to southern NGO; and
- the impact on relationships between southern NGOs and their northern counterparts.

The first phase included a review of NGO evaluation reports obtained from official agencies. In addition, a questionnaire was sent to the respective heads of the different NGO divisions of the major official donors or equivalent person. Where there were clear gaps in the information available (CIDA, USAID, EC), specific studies were commissioned. Interviews were carried out with NORAD and SIDA. Several major multilateral agencies were visited to update an earlier INTRAC study of their interaction with NGOs. Where necessary, follow-up questions were discussed with heads of northern NGOs as well as desk officers.

Case studies, covering three continents for comparative purposes, were selected. Country selection was made on the basis of evidence of a significant volume of direct funding, the frequency of the country's appearance in the priority country lists produced by official agencies and the existence of a well-developed local NGO community. In the case of Bangladesh, because of the relatively long history of direct funding, there was more research material than in Peru and Kenya.

Case studies included interviews with embassies or representatives of funding agencies in the countries to compile a list of local NGOs receiving direct funding. A few NGOs who had rejected direct funding were also interviewed. On average, thirty-five NGOs in each country with experience of direct funding were interviewed. In each country a workshop was held to convey the findings to, and to obtain comments from a representative NGO group.

A donor consultation (official agencies and northern NGOs) was held in Copenhagen during October 1996. This consultation was designed to inform representatives from various donor agencies of the findings of the case studies. The keynote speakers were the authors of the southern case studies. Their findings were discussed and the implications for the two main groups of participants were reviewed in working groups. This was well attended by four bilateral agencies, four multilateral agencies and fourteen northern NGOs.[1]

---

[1] See INTRAC (1996), *Changing Relations between Donors and Southern NGOs*, for more detailed information, including a list of participants.

Appendix 2

Trends in Official Aid to the NGO Sector in the 1990s

Donor	Trends in aid contributions	Funds to NGOs	Other comments
SIDA	Total aid allocations declined from US$2,460 million in 1992 to US$1,968 million (13,360 million Swedish Krone) in 1996. In 1996 development aid amounted to 0.82% of GNP, nearing its lowest level for 20 years.	The proportion provided to NGOs has increased from 12% of total disbursements in 1992–3 to 13.2% in 1996–7. In 1996 the proportion disbursed through direct funding to southern NGOs was 3.5%.	Most direct funding is provided to Bangladesh, India and Sri Lanka, increasing from SEK28 million in 1990 to SEK40 million in 1995 for these three countries.
DANIDA	Contributions exceeded 1% of GNP in 1996, rising from US$1.3 billion in 1993 to US$1.8 billion in 1996 (of which 50% is allocated to UN agencies).	Funds provided to Danish NGOs have grown, and in 1995 amounted to 16.5% of the bilateral budget.	Direct funding was introduced by DANIDA in 1988, and in general has been set at 10% of total aid financing for any individual country.
NORAD	Official aid contributions have remained stable during the 1990s at about 8,500 million Norweigian Kroner (or US$1,300), although as a percentage of GNP this represents a slight decline to 0.85% in 1996 from 0.87% in 1995.	The proportion of aid for NGOs has remained stable at 16–17% of the total. The proportion disbursed through direct funding has declined from 16% in 1994 to 12.7% in 1996. Primary support to southern NGOs has been through Norwegian NGOs, whose share of total NORAD funding to NGOs has risen from 81.1% in 1994 to 85.5% in 1996.	Growth in direct funding to southern NGOs occurred between 1981 and 1994, with disbursements rising from US$250 thousand in 1981 to US$14.5 million in 1993. Since then there has been strong opposition to direct funding in Norway.

Donor	Trends in aid contributions	Funds to NGOs	Other comments
DFID	British aid contributions declined during from 0.31% of GNP in 1994 to 0.25% in 1997.	Resources to NGOs provided through the Joint Funding Scheme has grown from £28 million in 1992–3 to £36 million in 1995–6. 24% of DFID expenditure is channelled through UK NGOs, through the Joint Funding Scheme mechanism. Direct funding to southern NGOs has also grown.	Small amounts of funds are disbursed directly to NGOs through British embassies (mainly in South Asia, Kenya and South Africa). DFID's bilateral programme has made substantial grants to a small number of large southern NGOs: BRAC (in Bangladesh) received US$12 million between 1991 and 1993, AKRSP (in Pakistan) received US$5.7 million between 1987 and 1991. Smaller NGOs have also received funds from the bilateral programme through NGO consortia: for example, the Bangladesh Population and Health Consortium, comprising 40 local NGOs, began with a three-year grant of US$3.4 million in 1988.
USAID	USAID disbursements have declined during the 1990s, from US$11,709 million (or 0.18% of GNP) in 1992 to US$9,058 million (or 0.12% of GNP) in 1996. Direct funding has grown from US$184 million in 1991 to US$307.8 million in 1995.	The proportion of funds provided to the NGO sector (Private Voluntary Organisations and southern NGOs) increased from US$496 million in 1991 to US$675.5 in 1995, of which approximately one-third was directed to southern NGOs during this period.	US Vice-President, Al Gore, pledged at the 1995 Social Summit that the US government 'would seek to channel up to 40% of its assistance to poor countries through private aid and charity groups that have demonstrated greater efficiency than many international organizations including the United Nations' (*Washington Post*, 13 March 1995).

Donor	Trends in aid contributions	Funds to NGOs	Other comments
CIDA	Overall aid disbursements have declined from US$2,515 million in 1992 to US$1,782 million in 1996.	CIDA's funding to NGOs through its Canadian Partnership Branch provided CAD$251 million to the voluntary sector in 1990–1, but by 1996 this had been reduced to CAD$199 million. As a percentage of total aid disbursements, this represents a small increase from 8.3% to 9.5%.	Because CIDA includes in its definition of the 'voluntary sector' support to universities, colleges and professional organisations, figures do not provide an accurate reflection of the size of commitments to NGOs. CIDA has provided substantial grants to support certain larger NGOs in the South directly from its Bilateral Programme, one of the first being Proshika in Bangladesh. Small grants for southern NGOs have been made available through the Canada Fund administered by Canadian embassies, and some funds from its bilateral programmes also provide support for NGOs. Counterpart funds have also provided resources to southern-based NGOs.
EC	European Commission development assistance budget has grown rapidly from US$1,244 million in 1980–1 to US$7,100 million in 1995.	The EC began funding European development NGOs in 1976 with an allocation of 2.5 million ECU, and the programme has grown substantially since, reaching 803 million ECU in 1994. Most EC funds have been directed through co-financing instruments, which had a budget of 160 million ECU in 1996. There has been a growing number of new sectoral	In principle, southern NGOs have access to funds under certain line items of the EC budget, but with a few notable exceptions, few southern NGOs have been able to obtain funds, partly as a consequence of the cumbersome procedures involved. There has been a tendency for the EC to fund only large NGOs which are already strong, such as BRAC and Proshika. Although several attempts have been made to

Donor	Trends in aid contributions	Funds to NGOs	Other comments
		budget line items established with funds accessible by NGOs. For example, the umbrella 'Food Aid' budget line amounted to 529 million ECU in 1997.	provide funds directly to NGOs in the ACP countries under the Lomé convention, few grants have in fact been made.
UN	Between 1990 and 1995 expenditure by UN Specialised Agencies increased by 41%. Spending by Specialized Agencies represents 39% of total on peacekeeping, agencies and regular expenditures. The four agencies emerging as key players in terms of spending on complex emergencies are the UNHCR, WFP, UNICEF and UNDP.	Most United Nations Development Programme (UNDP) representatives have a modest sum available for the direct funding of NGOs under the Participatory Development Programme (PDP) fund which has risen from US$25,000 per annum to approximately US$60,000 per country per year, since its inception in 1988. The PDP now operates in 77 countries through a locally constituted project committee made up of representatives of the UNDP, government officials and NGOs. In certain countries (e.g. The Gambia, Sri Lanka and Senegal) significant funds have been channelled from UNDP to local NGOs under the normal country programme funds, but this is very dependent upon local government acquiescence.	Other funds include: • General Environmental Facility, a small grants fund for environmental protection and bio-diversity which is working in 10–15 countries with an annual budget of US$200,000 per country. • The Africa 2000 Fund provides funds for rural development and environmental projects, giving in the region of US$200,000 per country. • The Asia-Pacific 2000 Fund is directed at urban areas, supporting projects in cities such as Manila, Delhi and Bangkok. • The Indicative Programme Fund (IPF) makes funds available to NGOs in agreement with the host government.

Donor	Trends in aid contributions	Funds to NGOs	Other comments
World Bank	The World Bank provides the vast majority of its development assistance to governments in the form of loans and NGOs do participate in some loan projects.	Since 1986 the Bank has funded NGOs directly, through its Social Funds. These are small grants made to support activities designed to promote dialogue, and are in the range of US$10–15,000. In 1995 the World Bank made awards totalling US$500,000 to 40 organisations world-wide. In the same year, southern NGOs received 80% of the total.	The Bank calculated that Social Funds accounted for over US$1 billion in new World Bank Group lending in 1997 and the approach is being generalised to most areas of World Bank Group interventions.

Sources: OECD 1996a; Cox and Koning 1997; NGO Handbook 1997; Pratt and Stone 1994. Global Policy web site-http://www.globalpolicy.org/finance/tables/tabsyst.htm

Bibliography

ADAB/PACT (n.d.) *Directory of Donors to Small NGOs in Bangladesh* (ADAB/PACT).

Bennet, J., and Gibbs, S. (1994) *NGO Funding Strategies* (Oxford: INTRAC).

Bratton, M. (1989) 'Beyond the State: Civil Society and Associational Life in Africa', in World Politics, 41.

Clark, J. D. (1991) *Democratising Development: The Role of Voluntary Organisations* (West Hartford, CT: Kumarian Press).

Cox, A., and Koning, A. (1997) *Understanding European Community Aid: Aid Policies, Management and Distribution Explained,* (London: Overseas Development Institute).

DFID (1997) *British Aid Statistics 1992/3–1996/7* (Government Statistical Service, East Kilbride).

Edwards, M., and Hulme, D. (eds.) (1992) *Making a Difference: NGOs and Development in a Changing World* (London: Earthscan).

Edwards, M., and Hulme, D. (eds.) (1995) *Non-Governmental Organisations, Performance and Accountability: Beyond the Magic Bullet* (London: Earthscan).

FEMNET (1989) *The Status of Voluntary and Non-profit Sector in Kenya* (Nairobi: A FEMNET Study)

Fowler, A. (1993) 'Non-governmental Organisations and the Promotion of Democracy in Kenya', Ph.D. thesis, Institute of Development Studies, University of Sussex, University Microfilms International (Ann Arbor, Mich.: University Microfilms International).

Fowler, A. (1994) 'Capacity Building and NGOs: A Case of Strengthening Ladles for the Global Soup Kitchen?' *Institutional Development*, 1/1: 18-24 (New Delhi: Society for Participatory Research in Asia).

Fowler, A. (1995) 'NGOs and the Globalisation of Social Welfare: Perspecitives from East Africa', in J. Semboja and O. Therkildsen (eds.) *Service Provision Under Stress: States and Voluntary Organisations in Kenya, Tanzania and Uganda* (London: James Curry).

Fowler, A. (1996) 'Strengthening the Role of Voluntary Development Organisations: Nine Policy Issues Facing Official Aid Agencies', in *Strengthening Civil Society's Contribution to Development: The Role of Official Development Assistance* (New York/Washington: Synergos Institute and the Overseas Development Council).

Freire, P. (1970) *The Pedagogy of the Oppressed* (Harmonsworth: Penguin).

Githu, K. (1995) *The Role of the Donors in Kenya's Development.*

Harper, C. (1996) 'Strengthening Civil Society in Transitional South East Asia', in A. Clayton (ed.) *NGOs Civil Society and the State: Building Democracy in Transitional Societies* (Oxford: INTRAC).

Howes, M., and Sattar, M. G. (1992) 'Bigger and Better? Scaling-up Strategies Pursued by BRAC 1972–1991', in M. Edwards and D. Hulme (eds.) *Making a Difference: NGOs and Development in a Changing World* (Earthscan: London).

Ikiara Gerrishon, K., and Tostensen, A. (1995) *The Political Economy of Poverty Reducation in Kenya,* a consultancy report for SIDA (June) (Nairobi).

Krystal, A., Waithaka, D., and Young, S. (1995) 'NGOs in Kenya: A Review', Report of a Study for SIDA (Nairobi: Matrix Development Consultants).

Liaison Committee of Development NGOs to the European Union (1997) *NGO Handbook 1997: Practical Information for Development and Emergency Aid NGOs in the European Union* (Brussels).
Malena, C. (1997) *NGO Involvement in World Bank-Financed Social Funds: Lessons Learned*, Environment Department Papers No. 052 (World Bank).

Muchunguzi, D., and Milne, S. (n.d.) *Perspectives From The South: A Study On Patrnership* (AFREDA).

Ndegwa, S. N. (1993) 'NGOs as Pluralizing Agents in Civil Society in Kenya', Institute of Development Studies Working Paper no. 491, (June) (University of Nairobi).

Ng'ethe, N., and Kanyinga, K. (1992) *The Politics of Development Space: The State amd NGOs in the Delivery of Basic Services in Kenya*, Working Paper No. 486, Institute of Development Studies, University of Nairobi (June).

NGSO Concerns (1991) *Concerns and Recommendations of the NGOs on the NGO Co-ordination Act* (February) (Nairobi).

Ngungi, M. G., and Gathaika, K. (1993) 'State–Civil Institutions Relations in Kenya in the Eighties', in P. Gibbon (ed.), *Social Change and Economic Reform in Africa* (Uppsala: Scandinavian Institute for Africa).

NORAD (1996) *Annual Report 1996*.

Nyangira, N. (1987) 'Ethnicity, Class and Politics in Kenya', in G. Schartzberg (ed.), *The Political Economy of Kenya* (New York: Prager Publishers).

ODA (1995) *British Aid to Kenya: General Briefing* (British Development Division in East Africa (March).

ODI (1995) *NGOs and Official Donors*, Briefing Paper, (London) (August).

OECD (1996a) *Development Co-operation: Development Assistance Committee Report 1995* (Paris).

OECD (1996b) *Directory of Non-Governmental Organisations Active in Sustainable Development. Part One–Europe* (Paris).

Ongwen, O. (1996) *NGO Involvement in Socio-economic and Political Transformation in Kenya after Independence*, Paper prepared for Workshop between Human Rights NGOs and Representatives of Donor Agencies (Nairobi), (11–12 April).

Osodo, P., and Matsvai, S. (1998) *Partners or Contractors? The Relationship between Official Agencies and NGOs: Kenya and Zimbabwe*, INTRAC Occasional Paper No. 16 (Oxford: INTRAC).

Peck, L., and Schill, G. (1996) *Direct Support to Southern NGOs*, Final Report (SIDA Asia Department) (Stockholm).

Pinzas, T. (1997) *Partners or Contractors? The Relationship between Official Agencies and NGOs – Peru*, INTRAC Occasional Paper No. 15 (Oxford: INTRAC).

Pratt, B., and Stone, A. (1994) *Multilateral Agencies and NGOs*, INTRAC Occasional Paper No.1 (Oxford: INTRAC).

Randel, J., and German, T. (1996) *The Reality of Aid: An Independent Review of International Aid*, ICVA, Eurostep (London: Earthscan).

Randel, J., and German, T. (1997) *The Reality of Aid: An Independent Review of International Aid*, ICVA, Eurostep, Actionaid (London: Earthscan).

Riddell, R., and Bebbington, A. (1995) *Developing Country NGOs and Donor Governments: Report to the ODA* (London: Overseas Development Institute).

Rutherford, S. (1995) *ASA: The Biography of an NGO* (Dhaka: ASA).

Sanyal, B. (1991) 'Antagonistic Cooperation: A Case Study of Non-governmental Organisations, Government and Donors in Income-Generating Projects in Bangladesh', *World Development*, 15 Supplement.

SIDA (1996a) *Swedish Development Co-operation with Kenya*, Memo from the Development Co-operation Section of the Swedish Embassy (Nairobi) (May).

SIDA (1996b) *Sweden's International Development Co-operation: Statistical Yearbook 1996* (Stockholm: Division for Financial Control).

Smillie, I. (1995) *The Alms Bazaar. Altruism under Fire – Non-profit Organizations and International Development* (Exeter: IT).

Smillie, I. (1998, forthcoming) 'At Sea in a Sieve', in I. Smillie and H. Helmich (eds.) *Stakeholders: Government – NGO Partnerships for International Development* (Paris: OECD).

Smillie, I. and Helmich, H. (1993) *Non-governmental Organisations and Governments: Stakeholders for Development* (Paris: OECD).

Smilie, I., Douchamps, F., Sholes, R., and Covey, J. (1996) *Partners or Contractors? Official Donor Agencies and Direct Funding Mechanisms: Three Northern Case Studies: CIDA, EU and USAID*, INTRAC Occasional Paper No. 11 (Oxford: INTRAC).

Sobhan, B. (1997) *Partners or Contractors? The Relationship between Official Agencies and NGOs – Bangladesh* INTRAC Occasional Paper No. 14 (Oxford: INTRAC)

Sobhan, R. (ed.) (1990) *From Aid Dependence to Self Reliance: Development Options for Bangladesh* (Dakha: BIDS-UPL).

Stewart, S. (1997) 'Happy Ever After in the Market Place: Non-Governmental Organisations and Uncivil Society', *Review of African Political Economy*, 71: 11–34.

Tordoff, W. (1994) 'Political Liberalisation and Economic Reform in Africa', *Democratisation*, 1/1: 100–15.

Tvedt, T. (1995) *Non-Governmental Organisations as Channels in Development Assistance: The Norwegian System* (Oslo: Ministry of Foreign Affairs).

USAID (1996) *'Coping with Change' USAID/Kenya's Strategic Plan for the Fiscal Tears 1996–2000* (Nairobi) (February).

Valderrama, M. (1997) *New Directions in International Co-operation: A View from Latin America* (Oxford: INTRAC) (Originally published in Spanish as *Peru y America Latina: en el Nuevo Panorama de la Cooperacion Internacional* (Peru: CEPES).

Waithaka, D., and Glaesor, E. (1991) *Profiles in Sustainability: Practical Applications in Kenya,* Report to USAID PVO Co-financing Project of the NGO Sustainability Workshop held in Thika (Kenya).
Weiss, T., and Gordenker, L. (eds) (1996) *NGOs, the UN & Global Governance* (Boulder: Colo.: Lynne Rienner).

Wolfe, A. (1989) *Whose Keeper? Social Science and Moral Obligations* (Berkeley, Ca.: University of California Press).

Wood, A. (1994) *An Analysis of the Overseas Development Administration Proposal to Directly Fund Southern NGOs,* MSc Thesis, University of London.

Wood, G. D., (1993) *Seeking Power in the Society: An NGO's Approach to Social Mobilisation and Legal Rights in Bangladesh*, Occasional Paper 02/93 (Centre for Development Studies, University of Bath).

Wood, G. D. (1994) *Bangladesh: Whose Ideas, Whose Interests?* (Dhaka: UPL).